Stephen 'Hippie Kushi' Cox has lived an interesting life. After leaving home at 16 due to a difficult childhood, he took refuge with some 'artistic' friends at a squat in London's King's Cross.

Following a brief stint working as a rent boy in Earl's Court, a lucky break led to an initial career in catering back in Brighton, where he made some great friends.

When a good friend took a job in London, Stephen decided to flat share with him, after being offered a job at the BBC and ITV studios.

A few years later, a chance of a lifetime fell in his lap; he signed up to work as a teacher in The Gambia for a year. This experience then resulted in a complete change of career. At the age of 45, Stephen went to university to study psychotherapy. Sadly, soon after graduating, he was diagnosed with a serious health condition, leading to some challenging years.

But then, he discovered Goa and the wonderful hippie scene there, and everything changed forever.

For Mary and Richard Sutcliffe, what would life be without you and Whirl-y-Gig?

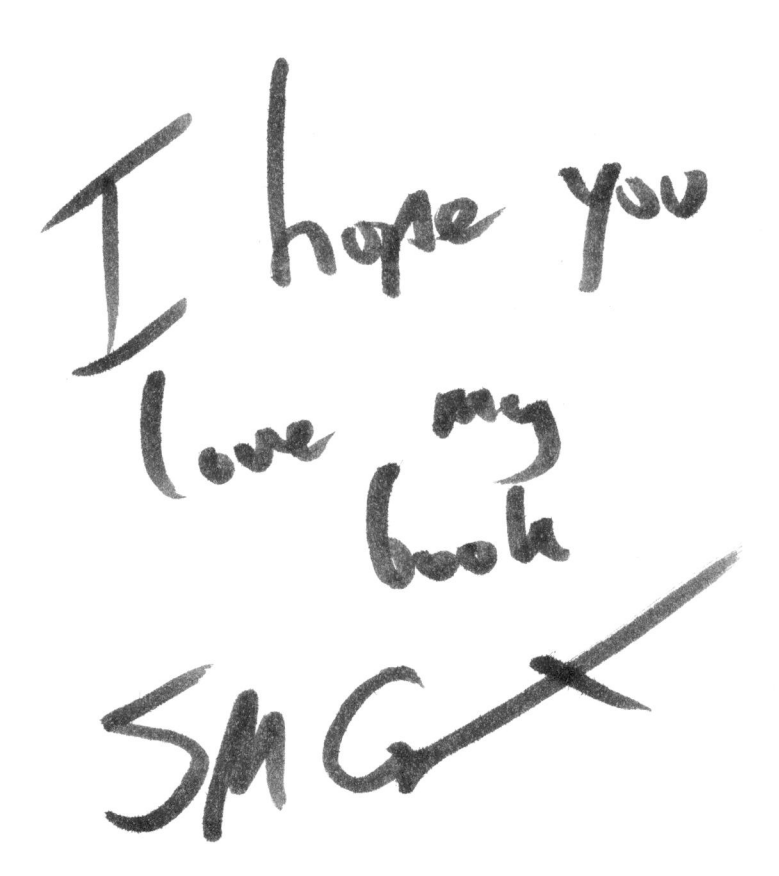

I hope you love my book
SMG x

Stephen 'Hippie Kushi' Cox

Hippie Kushi Waking up to Life

How to wake up from a full-stop life and find hippie happiness

Austin Macauley Publishers™

LONDON • CAMBRIDGE • NEW YORK • SHARJAH

Copyright © Stephen 'Hippie Kushi' Cox 2022

The right of Stephen 'Hippie Kushi' Cox to be identified as author of this work has been asserted by the author in accordance with section 77 and 78 of the Copyright, Designs and Patents Act 1988.

All rights reserved. No part of this publication may be reproduced, stored in a retrieval system, or transmitted in any form or by any means, electronic, mechanical, photocopying, recording, or otherwise, without the prior permission of the publishers.

Any person who commits any unauthorised act in relation to this publication may be liable to criminal prosecution and civil claims for damages.

All of the events in this memoir are true to the best of author's memory. The views expressed in this memoir are solely those of the author.

A CIP catalogue record for this title is available from the British Library.

ISBN 9781398402201 (Paperback)
ISBN 9781398402218 (Hardback)
ISBN 9781398443754 (ePub e-book)
ISBN 9781398420670 (Audiobook)

www.austinmacauley.com

First Published 2022
Austin Macauley Publishers Ltd®
1 Canada Square
Canary Wharf
London
E14 5AA

Thank you to Geoff Sarbutt and Mary Sutcliffe for taking the time to write the forewords for this book. Your kind words melted my heart.

"Everyone has the potential to change their life, surroundings and happiness!"

— Lillian Joyce

What if I fall? Oh, but my darling, what if you *fly*?

Foreword By
Geoff Sarbutt and Mary 'The Faery' Sutcliffe

Geoff Sarbutt:

'In many ways Stephen's story of life broadly matches my own – only the finer details and timescale differ.

I was a child of the '50s and hit the '60s as a teenager becoming immersed in the feelings of that time, but, as time passed, I became engrossed in my work life right up to my retirement. Maybe my younger days were a little more sedate than Stephen's and my working years did have some periods of life to them. After my retirement I started to rediscover things from my earlier life. To illustrate my time in the '90s at the Whirl-y-gig, I searched online in the hope of finding some old images, as I had assumed the Whirly had ended years earlier. To my surprise, the Whirl-y-Gig popped up and was still running – within seconds I booked a ticket for the next event.

I came across a link to Stephen's blog just before his first return to the Whirl-y-Gig. So much of his blog matched my own life; he had rediscovered the Whirly, he loved going to Goa, he aspired to living on a houseboat and he had worked at one time in the same organisation as me. I lived on a houseboat for eight years in the '80s and I have been going to Goa every winter for the past fifteen years. With at least some things in common I introduced myself to him when he made his first return to the Whirly.

The wonderful thing that I have discovered in my retirement years, is that, us children of the '60s are breaking the tradition of earlier generations by refusing to become "old" and not fitting into the classic old person's lifestyle. I hope Stephen's book will give an insight into this and encourage others of our generation to get out there and be involved in whatever way suits them.'

About Geoff: Geoff is like a guru to me; he has certainly lived a life of adventure. Now retired and still going strong, I met Geoff on my first visit to Whirl-y-Gig and we immediately clicked. You will find out more about Geoff as this book goes on – but let's just say, Geoff is a fountain of knowledge, colourful and a larger-than-life character

Mary Sutcliffe:

'Stephen's inspiration is the key to the faery realms. Thank you, Balloon Man, for leading us along that rainbow road to find the beauty and joy we all deserve. Thank you for going with the flow, for showing us how to live rather than exist, how to connect with our souls and watch the magic of possibility unfold.'

About Mary: Mary Sutcliffe is one of the organisers, leading lights and host of Whirl-y-Gig alongside her husband, Richard Sutcliffe, aka DJ Monkey Pilot. Whirl-y-Gig is a unique clubbing experience that has been going for over 38 years and is more like a way of life.

Mary says of herself: I am Fae and live in this real and beautiful world with all its conflict and its joy. I believe that we are all Fae, all magical beings and that everything is possible. I make contributions whenever I can, particularly through music and through continuing to love and follow Goddess in all Her nature – the earth, sun, moon, wind, sky, fire, water – all living creatures and all people. I trained at Glastonbury Goddess Temple and am a Priestess of Avalon. I am a multi-instrumental music teacher and run bi-weekly Whirly music events and an annual festival with my beautiful husband and a variety of other Goddess-inspired happenings. I spread the love of Rhianon. I was born in Faeryland, West Yorkshire and am the seventh child of seven sisters and seven brothers. Our parents were musicians who understood the meaning of real magic, that which comes from nature, the joy of togetherness and the music of life (taken from her Facebook page).

*

My Ten Steps to Hippie Kushi Happiness:

1. Look at the best parts of your life and rekindle them.
2. Travel the world and visit India – especially Goa.
3. Dance, dance and dance to wonderful music with other like-minded people.
4. Regularly attend Whirl-y-gig and Whirl-y-Fayre (if at all possible); it will change your life.
5. Regularly attend festivals.
6. Change your mind-set – the way you look and the way you live your life.
7. Embrace life and expand your hippie consciousness.
8. Love your fellow man (and woman) and your planet.
9. Live an alternative lifestyle.
10. Live a life full of Hippie Kushi; doing what you want to do!!!

*

Introduction

To the Vale of Avalon the Whirlys did come
For four days of mirth, dancing and fun
Below the old Tor the fayre had begun

In a green field in Somerset
under a clear blue sky
the colourful people were learning to fly

The spirits and faeries were having such fun
Joining hands with the hippies
To the beat of a drum

"In my living room, looking through the window across the balcony and courtyard into the trees, I pictured all the beautiful places there are in the world to visit. Somewhere, deep inside me, the idea percolated that it was time to run from the madness of conventional existence.

My attempt at developing a 'mainstream' lifestyle was doomed. Like everyone else, my ultimate desire was to find happiness. Surely this existed for me somewhere in the world." Bedroll, Bushes and Beaches – The Hippie Years – Ron White

Most people as they get older tend to forget about themselves. It seems to be a normal part of the process of life and it happens to the best of us. We forget to reach our own potential because we are far too focused on bringing up a family, working long hours to pay off the mortgage and bills, locked into the cycle of the never-ending treadmill of work and career. It is easy to lose our way and disregard our own existential wellbeing.

It is an undeniable fact that many of us, in later life, become a bit stuck.

Suddenly, one day thirty years later, we say to ourselves; 'What happened to the person I used to be, what happened to my life?'

We used to be fun, go to parties, dance the night away at night clubs and have loads of crazy friends, but the clubs and festivals of old have now been replaced by a pint at the local pub or wine and nibbles at your neighbour's house. Live music concerts have been replaced by a night at the theatre every few months, or worse still, and this is my own personal experience, your social life consists of a bottle of wine at home watching TV. Our friends are becoming fewer and fewer because over the years we have focussed on everybody else except ourselves; namely our family and our career.

My name is Stephen 'Hippie Kushi' Cox – I am 55 years old and I would happily describe myself as a hippie. I am both spiritual and forward-thinking, a traveller of the world and a lover of life. I embrace people of all cultures and I believe in togetherness and multiculturalism. I paint my brow with the colours of the rainbow, I wear bright multi-coloured clothes, beads and I dance with my whirly friends all through the night. I am HAPPY!!! I have found hippie happiness, I have found Hippie Kushi and I would love it if you could too.

I now embrace many new things in my life and have rekindled some old passions as well. I enjoy listening to great world music, especially at live gigs. I love dancing at clubs and festivals and I adore sleeping under the canvas in the beautiful British countryside. I have found deep joy dancing with other crazy hippies on the beaches of Goa in India. Travelling abroad has resulted in me meeting new, interesting and exciting people. In Anjuna and Arambol I have danced myself into total elation to the sound of fantastic world music, Drum n Bass and psytrance. Yes, I said psytrance – believe me, you will love it too when you see the happy whirly freaks, global nomads, new age warriors and woodland faeries dancing to those happy uplifting beats.

Through my world travel's and through spiritualism, meditation, music, Whirl-y-Gig, Parlour Party, Whirly-Fayre, festivals and my wonderful and exciting new friends, I have found a new lust for life and I have never been happier.

But things have not always been like this.

How do we find ourselves living out these stagnant grey years, where our life has ground to a full-stop? When did we start forgetting about who we are and the possibilities our lives could hold? When did we go from being young at heart to being old and boring?

I went through a long period in my life where I was stuck and I was living a full-stop life. The years seemed to pass by in a blur – I had a few friends, I was working crazy long hours at the NHS and my social life was non-existent. I was lost and had forgotten who I was. But a trip to Goa in India a few years ago changed my life forever and once I had found my lost mojo and the positive energy, I needed to transform myself like a butterfly emerging from a cocoon; I have not looked back.

*"And hand in hand, on the edge of the sand,
They danced by the light of the moon."*

— Edward Lear, The Owl and the Pussycat

Forget about age, you are never too old to let your hair down and have a wonderful time. In five years' time, I will be claiming my free bus pass but I feel more alive and feel more energised than ever before. I have embraced my true self and the hippie within me. My life is full of friendship and love, open-mindedness, spiritualism, music, laughter and dancing.

If you too feel you need that kick up the arse, it's time to 'WAKE UP TO LIFE' the Hippie Kushi way!

"And those who were seen dancing were thought to be insane by those who could not hear the music."

— Friedrich Nietzsche

So I guess the best place to start is with my own story, but just before I do that, I want to explain why the hippie ideal is so important to me and why in these days of Brexit, Donald Trump, Islamic terrorism, plastic waste and global warming, the hippie movement is making a comeback.

Chapter One
Hippie Happiness

Crazy Dancing Hippie People

"You've gotta dance like there's nobody watching,
Love like you'll never be hurt,
Sing like there's nobody listening,
And live like it's heaven on earth."

— William W. Purkey

Why My Fascination with Hippie Culture?

I was born in 1965 during the rise of the hippie phenomenon in America – but only being a baby at the time, I missed all the great events of that period. Somehow, though, that interest has always been there for me. One of my early friends, after I left school, was an interesting guy called Mathew Martis. He was always the trendy far-out one in our group of friends, loved listening to music artists like Nick Drake and Jimi Hendrix and introduced me to the hippie music I so love today, and things simply developed from there.

I remember one night at my house-share in Brighton, sitting with a two-litre bottle of cider watching the three-hour movie of the Woodstock concert; I was now totally smitten. This concert introduced me to Crosby, Stills and Nash and Neil Young – I still absolutely love them today. Then I saw the HAIR movie, a wonderful, uplifting concoction of hippie music and spirituality against a backdrop of the Vietnam War; still my favourite musical today.

My music collection grew and included groups such as A Loving Spoonful, The Byrd's, The Doors, Led Zeppelin, Love and Jefferson Airplane. Later, of course, I discovered the nightclub Whirl-y-Gig, a hippie paradise and my image started to match my love for all things hippie.

Many of the original hippies followed the hippie trail to India and the remnants of that society are still evident in Goa today. I love that social scene in Anjuna and Arambol and I embrace it – the freedom and lifestyle, the flower power and the music and most of all the love in this age of segregation and hate.

"What I mean by 'the hippie ideal' is the internal essence of the tribal feeling separate and apart from the external symbols which soon became overused, distorted, co-opted, and thus, understandably satirised. The conceit is that if you subtract long hair, hip language, tie-dyed clothing, beads, buttons, music, demonstrations, and even drugs, there was still a distinctive notion of what it meant to be happy and a good person, and a sense of connection to others was the invisible force behind things. It included the moral imperative to fight for civil rights and against the war, and the spiritual notion that there were deeper values than fame and fortune, peace and love."

— In Search of the Lost Chord 1967 and the idea – Danny Goldberg ICON books ltd 2017

The Hippie Ideal and Indian Culture

I have recognised over time, through in-depth reading and study into the Indian culture, but also as a consequence of my travels to India, why those original hippies found such a connection with the Indian continent, to its people, its spirituality and the ideals that shaped its very being.

The hippie ideal was one of community – looking after each other and working together to bring harmony and cooperation, creating a peaceful way of life whilst looking after every living thing on the planet. The hippies were often spiritual, some through Christianity but most with a more open-minded view of god and a need to explore other religions from around the world.

"Then, who were the hippies and what was the counterculture they represented… the hippie culture of the 1960s was a group of people who at first identified themselves by what they were not, and then engaged in a way of living that they believed would lead them down the path toward the creation of a New Age; a society and culture that was more humane, spiritual, and free than any that had existed before. Hippie philosophy stressed the need for pacifism, quietism, creativity, gratification, and community. Hippies translated these values into a radical break with mainstream society's institutions, culture, and lifestyle. Instead of aggression, destructive productivity, obscene commercialism, and conspicuous consumption, the hippie ethos affirmed peace, love, sensuousness, environmentalism, and a simple, less materialistic life. Hippies envisioned the ideal community as one where everyone was turned on and happy and floating free. Their goal wasn't one long party but rather to create a new society that integrated art and life."

— The Hippies, a 1960s History – John Anthony Morella.

Unfortunately, as time has passed, western culture's need for material things has led to an insular society, where individualism seems to rule the day. And this I believe, as well as the use of more hardcore drugs such as Heroin and Cocaine is why the original hippie movement lost its way and fizzled out.

But there were still many who held onto those principles and these hippies were the ones who followed the hippie trail to India. Still, today, new age travellers and modern-day hippies continue to travel to the Indian continent in search of spirituality and the ideals of oneness and community (even though these days most travellers prefer airline travel over travelling the now dangerous hippie trail through Afghanistan and Iran).

But why did they choose India over other places?

The Indian psyche is different from that of the West, especially so for those of the Hindu faith, but also in general. Indians believe in the oneness of family and community. They also see all other Indians as their family and believe that working as one brings the harmony they seek. The reward for this collaboration of souls is the achieving of dharma and karma (deeds). Hindus believe in reincarnation and each reincarnation is based on the deeds they achieved in their former lives.

"Karma is the Hindu belief that a person's destiny is determined by their actions while they are alive. If a person lives a life of righteousness, then they will live an even better life when they are reborn."

— Hinduism for Beginners – Shalu Sharma 2016

When you visit India, you will experience this feeling of oneness amongst the people and I believe that it is this that attracted the original hippies to this warm and friendly country, and still attracts similar minded people to make that trip today.

This is why I take such solace and comfort from the hippie ideal and happily call myself a modern-day hippie!

The Hippies Are Coming Back

It is certainly noticeable these days in Europe and the US how many people with the hippie look you can now see walking the streets of our cities. At festivals and clubs, you see them on mass. The hippie movement is returning to the world because once again the world is in disarray. People are talking about saving the planet, becoming vegan, attending political protests and embracing Eastern spirituality, religions, yoga and meditation, medicines and treatments.

Before the original hippie movement began, society, especially in the USA was in a mess. Racism and human rights abuses were prevalent. The shocking assassinations of Martin Luther King, JFK and Malcolm X and many others proved that hate and intolerance were on the rise throughout the world and all of this with the backdrop of the Vietnam War. These events paved the way for a new peace movement that went against all that darkness; the result was the hippies of the late 1960s.

Today, the world is in a similar mess, if not worse: Trump, Brexit, racism, intolerance and the threat of war with Iran, Russia or China. Global warming and the environment are a real worry for many people and we are becoming a materialist, isolationist and a nationalist society.

The seeds for change are being sewn, so it's no wonder the hippies are coming back; a modern version of them for certain but hippies none the less. Look around you, it won't take you long to spot us; we are growing in number; the freaks are on the rise.

Crazy Dancing Hippie People

Who are they? What do they do for money? Where do they live? How do they look? Where do they travel?

I believe the hippies of today are much more focused than their predecessors and they often use art as a way of spreading their message. This art comes in many forms – writing, art, photography, performance and music. Modern-day hippies are often keen writers, writing everything from fiction, self-help books, books on veganism and natural remedies and guides on eastern exercise such as Tia Chi; often writing books from a spiritual and political perspective. They are poets and songwriters, creative bloggers and social media savvy 'preachers of the hippie mind-set'.

Many often choose to live alternative lifestyles on canal boats or travelling around Europe in hippiefied campervans. Some live in community housing co-ops or in ramshackle caravans and tent communities.

Today's hippies produce beautiful crafts, clothes and jewellery selling their wares from market stalls. They are entertainers, performing as dancers, actors and circus performers, creating music in bands and as solo acts. They sit in drum circles on Asian beaches and DJ in hippie orientated clubs.

Their clothes are more colourful and outrageous than ever before, neon glow sticks and disco light goggles.

The new hippies love to travel; congregating in parts of Southern Europe, South East Asia and India, especially wonderful Goa.

They are spiritual and political with a newfound vigour at a time when the world is in chaos. They study Eastern religions and raise their hands up to Gaia. They march in protest against our foolish governments and weep at the sadness and insanity of the world's plight on so many levels.

They are often vegan and strongly support the environment and saving our wonderful planet.

And most of all they crave joy, they dance, they sing and they love.

There is a new dawn approaching, we cannot go on as we are. This new hippie movement is rising and God knows we need it right now.

So, are the new hippies so different from the 1960s hippies? Yes, I believe they are. They are more focused and have learnt from the mistakes of their 1960s predecessors.

A new hippie movement is coming; you only need to attend festivals like 'Into the Woods' and Whirly Fayre to see this growing trend.

The new hippie Kushi dawn is upon us.

*

Chapter Two
Whatever Happened to Mad Mary and the Balloon Man?

How did I become the character I am today? Was I always like this or did I evolve into it?

The truth is, I have always been a little eccentric – I just lost myself along the way.

When I was a young man, I was wild, eccentric and crazy. I was artistic and creative and held a fondness for hippie music and had a look that could only be described as 'colourful'. Being young and gay, I enjoyed going to clubs and parties (as most young people do) and I lapped up the club culture of the time, which happened to be the New Romantics. I think as a consequence of a difficult childhood, I wanted to show the world that I was somebody – I had great friends with shared interests and felt I could conquer the universe.

I travelled a lot too, especially to Amsterdam where I enjoyed the canals and the boats (a passion I still hold today). I also enjoyed the laid-back culture, and if I'm honest, smoking da-weed. I had a lust for life and those were some of the happiest days I can remember.

Back then, a gay man was often called a Mary by his friends, it was a funny way of saying you were a typical gay stereotype; camp and outlandish. Because of my crazy antics on the club scene, I was gifted with the nick-name Mad Mary, which I wore with pride. I frequented clubs such as the infamous Beacon Royal in Brighton and London's Heaven and G.a.y.

The first big change was when I shared a flat in North London with my lifelong friend Nick; he had travelled up from Brighton (my hometown) with me. We discovered a club called Whirl-y-Gig. It was a colourful hippie New Age paradise full of ageing hippies, bohemians, new age activists and long-haired hipsters (www.whirl-y-gig.org.uk). The club still exists to this day.

The Whirly club played all kinds of interesting and exciting music, including lots of world music beats and it was eccentric, colourful and laid back. They had bongo drummers, dancers and live bands and at the end of the night a huge parachute would be pulled above the crowd and hundreds of balloons would be floated over the top of it as it was lit with psychedelic lights; it was a moment to chill after a crazy night of dancing and the effect was amazing.

After being a regular for months, I was offered the role of 'Balloon Man' and my job was to blow up the balloons and give them out to the crowd ready for the parachute finale. I earned about £10 a night for this but it wasn't about the money. When you entered the club, a lady sat at the door and offered face painting, as I was the Balloon Man my face was painted each time, so I looked wild.

The crowd would see me coming and shout, "Balloon Man," and they would cheer and greet me; it was great.

I was sadly sacked from the role at the end because I gave too many balloons away to the party crowd early in the evening, leaving none for the parachute finale.

Whirl-y-Gig held open-air events too and my fondest memory of this time was a live concert event on Hampstead Heath. The crowd was huge, and it was like a scene from the '60s, full of spaced-out hippies; great music and lots of beer and weed.

After a while I moved on from this, I needed to work. I had left home young because of my violent father and had pretty much partied since I had left Brighton for London. I grew up a lot after that and Nick, me and my boyfriend, Trevor, moved to a flat in Brixton. My image changed too, I tamed it down a lot. I was very into Tom Waits at the time and my image mirrored this. I wore a cloth cap and sported a goatee. This was the first time I grew a beard and I have had one ever since.

I found work at the BBC as a catering assistant for many years; it didn't stop me going out though. The club scene was heating up with the arrival of techno music. Later, I got a bit hooked on the ecstasy scene that went with it and for about five years I clubbed every night. It became a problem in the end though and so, just like that, I stopped going to raves and never took E again for years.

My life began to change in stages, first I had a terrible break up with my Jamaican boyfriend, Trevor, when we were on holiday in New York; he had grown very possessive and physically violent. In a moment of anger on the flight home, I told him I never wanted to see him again, the strange thing was, I never did. He moved out and disappeared completely. Nick and I have never seen him on the scene or anywhere else in London to this day. We do not know what happened to him. It was the time when AIDS was at its worst and Trevor was a very promiscuous young guy, many of my friends had died of this terrible disease and I wondered if he had, too. I will probably never know.

Somehow, during that terrible time in the late '80s, early '90s I had not managed to catch that horrible virus, but it was a difficult time for everyone.

Trevor was the love of my life and I was heartbroken, I cried for weeks. As a result, I began looking for something new in my life, something to thrill me again. Strangely, this came through my catering career – I worked my way up to banqueting manager at a well-known university and we used to arrange conferences for foreign aid companies that provided schools and teachers to places like India and Africa. We provided catering for these conferences and I used to stand and listen to their speeches on how they would build schools in poor countries and then send volunteers on TEFL courses in Oxford before sending them off to these countries to work as teachers. I quickly signed up, left my job and the next thing I knew, I was on a flight to The Gambia in Africa for a year.

The school was in a remote jungle village called Kunkajang and there was no running water or electricity. The locals were so friendly and although poor, seemed to have all their needs met. They grew vegetables and kept livestock, so their food needs were taken care of. The locals were liberal Muslims (I say liberal because they drank beer and smoked weed) and they worked very much as a community, helping each other out and supporting each other; from building and mending houses to looking after the crops. I would have to travel to the community well for water and I used candles for light. The kids were just wonderful, all ages from six to sixteen and ready to learn; my year in Africa was wonderful and I didn't want to come back when it ended, but of course I had to.

Sadly, it was on my return to the UK that my life began to change and move in a negative direction. I began to move towards the grey full stop life I ended up living for over ten years. Of course, there were no fridges in the village in Africa and my daily meals consisted of half a bonga fish and rice. The rice would sit for days in the heat with flies swarming over it. When I got back to London my health was not good, my stomach was churning, and I felt unwell. When I came back to the UK homeless, I was put on the council housing list and ended up in temporary accommodation in Deptford. The place was a small room on a gang-ridden estate; it was horrible.

Because I needed to earn ASAP, I took a job at a Waitrose supermarket as a wine expert (who figured) and fell into a dull routine. One day at work I keeled over in pain and ran to the toilet. I could not stop being sick from that moment on and was rushed to hospital where I remained for three weeks. First of all, they thought I had malaria and kept me in isolation.

I had test after test until after a couple of weeks a doctor came in and sat on my bed and I noticed she had a strained look on her face.

She held my hand and said, "Stephen, you have AIDS!"

Of course, I was horrified, especially as she told me the lesions on my legs were a type of skin cancer; I was sure I was going to die. The funny thing is (every cloud) because of my condition I was gifted a council flat in Camberwell, so I did not have to deal with this in that hellhole in Deptford. I then felt I had to tell my close friends such as Nick about my condition. Nick is always there for me and always will be, I love him, he is like family and he was great about it, in fact, all my friends were very understanding.

As I am writing this book, it is obvious I didn't die. The medication these days is amazing, the cancer has disappeared, and my status changed from AIDS to HIV+ and my CD4 (white blood cell count) shot up to a safe level and my health went back to almost normal: almost. I did not realise it then, but my diagnosis would affect the rest of my life in different ways. The creation of new HIV medication has led to the wonder drug Truvada, which almost eradicates HIV in the body (as long as you keep taking it), which means the possibility of me infecting somebody else is now extremely low (if not zero) and my white blood cell count is higher than most healthy people.

I became proactive, then, I signed up to university at the age of 45 and studied to become a counsellor at Roehampton University. My experience at university was very positive and I have made good friends from those days. I also think it has helped me now in my new journey of exploration because I have a better understanding of myself. I qualified from university with a BSc 2.1 with honours in Psychotherapeutic Counselling (Psychotherapy) in 2013 and worked for a short while in private practice. With the recession, though, it was hard to find paying clients and I found myself slowly moving over to admin work for the NHS, which I still do to this day.

Two years ago, I got a transfer out of the rough estate I lived in Lambeth and moved to lovely Hampton in Surrey by the river with its canal boats that I so love.

It all sounded pretty good then, didn't it? Well, I am sorry to say it wasn't; my life had come to a full stop. My life was lacking in worth and the stigma of being HIV+ had ruined my romantic prospects as well as my love of myself and my body. I hardly saw my friends and was staying in at the weekend watching TV with a bottle of wine. I was crippled by credit card debt and was desperate to get out of the rat race and rekindle that old me; The 'me' that craved adventure and travel. But, due to depression, I found it hard to find the getup and go to climb out of this grey period and so it continued like this for a decade.

So, what happened to break me out of this rut, out of that grey full stop existence?

The answer is simple:

Goa!

Midlife Crisis or Awakening

Although this book is about my journey, I hope anyone who has experienced being a bit stuck in life can take something away from this. What follows is my own personal moment of Utsaah.

उत्साह /Utsaha/Utsaah

1. **Elation** – extreme happiness
2. **Enthusiasm** – uncountable noun
   Enthusiasm is great eagerness to do something or to be involved in something.
3. **Exuberance** – uncountable noun
   Semionova has the confidence and exuberance of youth.
4. **Spirit** – plural noun
   You can refer to your spirits when saying how happy or unhappy you are. For example, if your spirits are high, you are happy. Exercise will help lift his spirits.
5. **Verve** – uncountable noun
   Verve is lively and forceful enthusiasm.

He looked for the dramatic, like the sunset in this painting, and painted it with great verve. She revelled in big MGM musicals with their colour and verve.

6. **Vibrancy** – uncountable noun
   She was a woman with extraordinary vibrancy.

This was me in 2008, about two years before this photo was taken, I had returned from my long stint as a teacher in The Gambia, Africa. After a while, I felt I needed a holiday, I had always liked the Netherlands and had decided to take myself off to Amsterdam, a place where many years before I had found happiness. Amsterdam was fun and a little bit crazy… like I used to be.

The amazing adventure that I had had in Africa had awoken something in me but I had not recognised its significance until that trip to the Netherlands in 2008 when I was 43 years old. I was lost, unhappy and lonely. I had no partner and I had begun the unconscious defensive behaviour of losing myself in long hours of work rather than facing up to my unhappiness. In Amsterdam, I went to nightclubs I had enjoyed when I was younger, but once there, I felt out of place and isolated. I drank heavily and instead of enjoying the beautiful historic city, felt hung-over and rough. I smoked weed and instead of feeling peaceful and enlightened, I felt down and depressed. Amsterdam 2008 began my 'midlife crises'.

But why do we put ourselves into this box labelled 'midlife crisis?' What does that even mean? I now know that there was no 'crisis' involved because now in 2019, I have never been happier.

For years after that depressing trip to Amsterdam, I continued my behaviour of working long hours and staying in at weekends. I was living in my second rough housing estate at the time in Camberwell, South London, and often witnessed gang violence there. Then in 2015, I was given the opportunity to do a house swap with another housing association tenant and I moved to Hampton on the border of Surrey. It's quite rural and close to the river. I finally had the opportunity to relax my mind and take stock.

"So, what happened to you?"

This is a question I have been asked so many times when people hear about my adventurous past and see photos of my former exploits.

I reply, "I got old."

This, of course, is rubbish – I got scared, I got hooked on security and a safe existence and I started living a full stop life. I did not feel attractive anymore so I stopped dating. I got fat – "who wants to date a fat old gay man?" I started buying things I didn't need and got into debt with credit cards, as a result, I never had any money to travel (or so my mind-set told me).

The result of all this was losing myself in work. For years I worked up to ten hours a day for the NHS. I rarely went out to bars or clubs, although I have a good set of friends who I sometimes went to the theatre with or enjoyed home dinner parties, but I didn't get out there and meet new and exciting people. Often on weekends I would sit at home and get depressed.

But one day five years ago, I suddenly woke up. It all began when I read a life-changing book about travelling the world called: Vagabonding by Rolf Potts:

This book made me take a real hard look at myself. It is beautifully written and is not just about long-term travel but about our outlook on life and who we are; it really woke me up.

This inspirational book then found me looking for other books that would help me develop my new mind-set. One such book was about Hinduism. I have always been interested in this religion and this book built on this.

It was shortly after this that I had the dream.

The Dream

One Friday night, I was very tired, still working long hours, I was stressed as my landlord had threatened me with eviction if I missed another month's rent due to my credit card debt. I had been surprised by the strong reaction to something I thought was manageable.

I slept very well that night and sometime during my slumber the 'visit' happened. First of all, in my dream, I could see what appeared to be a rocky landscape but then I realised what I was seeing was skin, close up. But the skin was blue.

Then as the vision panned out, I could make out a smiling blue face, a handsome man with black eyeliner and a red mark in the centre of his forehead. His smile was warm and calming and he was looking straight at me.

"Who are you?" I asked.

"I am Vishnu," he replied.

I then said stupidly, "I thought Krishna was the blue one."

He laughed and said, "No. that's me, Vishnu, although, I am Krishna, too."

I began to say his name in my mind and then said: "Why are you here?"

He raised his hand, the palm flat and facing me. "I am here to watch over you."

"Why?" I asked, confused.

"Because, finally, you are starting on the right path."

Then I woke up, not sure if the dream had simply been a consequence of my reading that book about Hinduism. But I realised on waking up I felt well-rested and clear-headed; the best I had felt in ages. I now knew what I needed to do about my life and I made a plan.

Later, I looked up Vishnu, because I was not familiar with this particular Hindu god and sure enough, there he was; he is the BLUE one but it turns out Krishna is one of his avatars.

Vishnu

The 'All-Pervading' One.

In Hinduism, Vishnu, whose name means 'All-Pervading', is the protector of the world and the restorer of moral order (dharma). He is peaceful, merciful, and compassionate. To Vaisnavites, Vishnu is the Supreme Lord.

Vishnu is often pictured with his consort, Lakshmi (also called Sri), and usually has four arms. Each hand holds an emblem of his divinity: the conch, discus, club, and lotus. A curl of hair on his chest signifies his immortality, and he wears the jewel Kaustubha around his neck. He is usually depicted with a dark complexion, as are his incarnations. Vishnu is often shown reclining or asleep as he awaits the next annihilation and renewal of the world.

Vishnu is best known through his ten avatars (incarnations), which appear on earth when there is disorder in the world. Rama and Krishna, whose stories are told in the Epics and the Puranas, are the most popular incarnations of Vishnu by far. The ten incarnations of Vishnu are:

Matsya (fish) – Kurma (turtle) – Varaha (boar) – Narasimha (man-lion) – Vamana (dwarf) – Parashurama (warrior-priest) – Rama (prince) – Krishna (cow-herd) – Buddha (sage) – Kalki (horseman, who has not yet appeared).

http://www.religionfacts.com/vishnu

After my dream, I booked a flight to India.

Once I had arrived in Goa, I was changed forever!

Wanderlust, the Constant Dream; the Longing

"Today, I would never encourage anyone to travel around the world – alone or otherwise – because if you're cut out for such a trip, you don't need any spurs to your backside. There's already a beast within you – your own tiki god clawing at the door to get out – a compulsion you can't resist."

Planet Backpacker by Robert Downes, Wandering Press, 2008

During my lifetime I have travelled widely – I have travelled across America by Greyhound bus and I have taken another bus from London to Morocco. I have taken long train rides all across Europe, gone horse trekking through the swamps and jungles of Brazil and even had a stint of teaching in a remote village in Africa.

After a difficult childhood, I quickly found myself searching for more positive experiences. I used to fantasise about putting a backpack on and just going – just setting off to explore the world. I have since then travelled far and wide but even today I still have the wanderlust – I still dream of one day putting on a backpack and just going. I still have the constant dream; the longing; but the call is the strongest it's ever been.

"World travellers are driven by a spirit which the Greeks call daemon. Wanderlust, travelling' bone, travelling' Jones – call it what you like – but it's something that beats at your breast from the inside. Your daemon demands that you slave joyfully to the altar of your passion, be it music, art, writing, hunting, running, cooking, or grafting to the joystick of a PlayStation. Every hardcore traveller burns with this spirit – money doesn't matter and neither do the rough spots – it's making the trip that counts."

Planet Backpacker, 2008

The Full Stop Period

As previously stated, after my crazy years of partying, travelling and living the lifestyle that best suited who I was, I grew older and settled into a rather conservative and safe routine. I don't think there is anything wrong with this and many people, for whatever reason, end up becoming a bit boring as they get older; sometimes we just need a bit of a kick-start. Unfortunately, this kick-start is often misconstrued as a mid-life-crisis but I think it is more of a re-awakening, a re-identification of the person we really are underneath. Generally, family and responsibilities must have their time first before a new chapter can begin that frees you up to reorganise and refocus on who you really are and where you want to be.

If we look at existentialism psychology and the many interesting books and papers written around this subject (by people like Irvin Yalom), they often talk about life's 'chapters'. I totally get this concept and believe every chapter has its purpose and however difficult or dark some of those chapters may be, they serve to strengthen us and make us stronger and more resilient in the future.

There came the day when I woke up from what had become a full stop existence, a strange neutral chapter in my life, and the beginning of a whole new chapter began for me. This chapter in my life is still in its infancy but my hippie Kushi period began when I first visited India.

Hippie Kushi Waking Up to Life is a book that does what it says on the cover. It is about waking up and remembering who we really are. Embracing life, peace, freedom and happiness and going for it. One great way to expand your mind is through travel.

"On the other hand, I kept imagining myself on my deathbed, thinking – *Damn, I never did the one thing that I really wanted to do in my life...* followed by a ghastly urk!" — Planet Backpacker, 2008

Diary of the Journey That Changed My Life

I woke up from my strange slumber of life pretty much as soon as I arrived in India. I was in Goa and bouncing around in a taxi on my way to my hotel in Candolim, a typically touristy area of Goa. I was immediately struck by how different it was to anywhere else I have been. There were long-haired and bearded swami's (holy men) walking along the road with cows at their side that had been painted in bright colours and decorated with jewellery and bright cloth.

The place was full of thousands of Indians going about their daily business. Brightly coloured trucks beeped their horns as hundreds of scooters, heavily laden with all kinds of goods, moved back and forth across the road in all directions. In London, this scene would have stressed me out but in India, it seemed exciting and exotic.

My hotel room was basic but comfortable and the staff were very helpful and friendly. I decided to go out and buy a few essentials such as drinking water, and as I walked the streets, I started to see what can only be described as European 'hippies'. Men and women in baggy Indian pyjama trousers, with long hair or dreadlocks wearing brightly coloured beads.

This blew my mind and took me back to my hippie days when I was the balloon man at Whirl-y-Gig nightclub. I immediately homed in on a bar where a lot of these interesting chameleons were enjoying a drink. I thought, let's have a drink and ask them where they think the best places to hang out are. I should point out that at this stage, I was still in my boring, 'full stop life' stage, and was wearing a blue suit shirt, cream trousers and loafers. My hair was short and my goatee neatly trimmed.

I got a few strange looks when I asked my questions but it soon became evident that the best beaches for hippies were Anjuna and Arambol and that the best parties were the drum parties on Arambol beach, the Saturday night market and the Anjuna day market which then morphed into the Anjuna day market 'after party'.

So, after doing a few touristy things like visiting temples and a spice farm, I made my plans to attend these events.

The Saturday night market in Arpora came first (Arpora is a village close to the North Goa beach belt, in India's tourism-destination state).

Very famous for its night market, 'The Saturday Night Market', open during the tourist season, is a colourful vast market consisting of people from around the state selling and showcasing their goods. Be it the musical mouth harps or mouth-watering food, the variety is vast. I was totally blown away; the sights, the smells, the incredible food, the exotic, colourful characters, the ageing hippies, the comradery and friendship. People from all over the world were sitting, drinking and talking about life, spirituality and togetherness. And then the live music started and I was changed for life; I was in love with Goa from that moment. But it's hard to really express how amazing the night market is unless you experience it for yourself.

After the night market, I took a taxi to Arambol beach because I was told there were regular drum parties going on. The journey was hair-raising, as we narrowly missed speeding trucks coming from the opposite direction and weaved our way through jungle paths.

Arambol beach is the home of the hippies in Goa and some nights (and days), they get together on the beach and have these parties. The one thing that stood out for me was how at home I felt in this environment but how my persona did not match. I looked like an American tourist in my chinos and this was the first step in my deciding to reclaim my old identity. Boring Steve was fired!!!

Anjuna beach is another hippie beach and they often hold the famous Goa Trance parties there. I couldn't get into this music on my first visit to Goa but in subsequent visits, I have grown to love it.

The Day That Changed My Life

The day my life changed forever, when the real epiphany came, was the following Wednesday when I attended the day market in Anjuna and later the bars and clubs after this event.

I arrived at Anjuna beach by tuk-tuk and he dropped me off at the entrance to the beach. The ground was a red dust colour and the sun was not yet high in the sky which gave the place a spiritual feel. In order to walk down to the beach, you travel through a smaller local market and it was here I bought some Ganesh wall hangings for my bedroom back in the UK. The day was very hot and when I reached the beach with its beach shacks playing trance music, I quickly headed for the surf and threw off my sandals to walk along the sand with my feet in the cooling water.

You could hear the market before you reached it – the place was packed and the music was loud.

I made my way up a steep slope and entered the market. It was full of colourful stalls and there were hippie types everywhere. The stalls sold jewellery, drapes and statues of Hindu gods and all kinds of clothes and bags. I bought a load of fantastic hippie and Indian outfits because I knew my current look was on its way out; I was embracing this world. I heard that a lot of the older hippies who live in Goa make a living from selling clothes and jewellery at this market as well as the one in Arambol, but they constantly have to keep an eye out for the police as this is illegal for foreigners. There are rumours of hippies being beaten up and put in jail for this but they love the Goa lifestyle so much they take the risk. For some, paying a bribe to the cops is sometimes enough.

I then came across a bar/club playing live prog-rock music. I decided to go in, finding a well-positioned table by the stage I ordered a beer. Straight away a crazy drunk hippie lady from Brighton came and sat next to me and we made friends. We laughed and had a dance. Later more hippies arrived and sat with us and my life was changed forever; I wanted this.

Later on, in the evening I came back and went to the same bar. It was now a full-on night club and I danced all night with those crazy hippies. At least I had my hippie t-shirt to wear even if my hair was a bit square. I will never forget that day.

Sadly soon after, it was time to fly home but when I came back to the UK, I found my outlook had changed, I felt driven and positive. Soon after I started my blog and began the process of achieving my dreams.

"There is, perhaps, the risk of being loved; of opening your heart and letting others in. Your expectations of how happy you have any right to be might be threatened when you discover what fun it is to dance barefoot to the sound of a drum."

Planet Backpacker 2008

The Constant Dream, the Longing

"It was on that trip that I first became aware that there is an alternative world of gypsy travellers paralleling our own. You would seldom – if ever – meet them in the ordinary, workaday world, but as soon as you hit the road, the portals would open, revealing the oddest people, along with young adventurers heading for distant horizons."

Planet Backpacker 2008

My trip to India reignited my former love for travel, a love I had pushed aside during my 'full-stop' years; now I want more and more adventures like this. So, needless to say, the wanderlust had never really gone away, it had now become stronger than ever. I decided I would really like to spend longer and longer in Goa amongst my hippie friends and I would also love to don that backpack one day and just travel the world. The constant dream, the longing was suddenly reignited!

*

Soon after returning from Goa a changed man, I had another strangely spiritual experience. With a strong interest in Eastern religion, I have often meditated; especially when I'm feeling blue. On one such occasion I had had the flu and was feeling pretty rough, so I put on some of Brian Eno's ambient sounds (Ambient 1: Music for Airports) and laid flat on my back and controlled my breathing to relax. Normally my mind was so jumbled with negative thoughts and money worries I could not settle into a full meditative state but on this occasion, I did and I felt myself sink into a deep and peaceful place. Feeling beautifully calm I felt as though I was touched by an energy that said: enough!

My mind felt the clearest it had ever been and I was able to start planning in my mind what I had to do to escape my full-stop life and wake up to something more.

My first priority was to get out of debt – to make a plan to pay off my credit cards. I went straight on to that and this is now nearly dealt with, thanks to the help of Citizens Advice and a debt relief order; from December 28th 2019, I will be debt-free!

Then there was my work-life balance. I was 52 years old for god's sake, I wanted my life back. It's taken me a long time to change my work habits –

working long hours (70 hours a week) was what I was used to and I continued on this destructive treadmill at the NHS for far too long, even though it was making me sick and rundown. I had no time for my own stuff and I felt my life was not my own.

I have now finally left the NHS and have moved to a sports and fitness centre nearer to home, so no more of those three-hour commutes. This has resulted in me opening up time for my own artistic projects and I now find myself feeling peaceful and rested.

To add to all of this, I have also signed up to learn to drive a car (or van in my case), as I have never learnt to drive. It's a scary prospect but something that would open up a lot of doors for me. This would serve as a good means of transport when I start my own business and would offer me more independence. Eventually, when I am ready, I plan to buy a campervan, do it up and move into it, providing me with the extra funds (due to not paying high rent and bills) that would allow me to pay for my future long term vagabonding travels and eventually pay for that canal boat I have dreamed of living on my whole life, but more about this lifelong dream later.

Then, of course, there are the travels themselves. Embracing my inner hippie, I want to travel to places where I can find this hippie spirit as well as awakening my spiritual side. So, that means countries like Thailand, India, Vietnam, Cambodia and so many more wonderful places and I cannot wait!

All these plans seem like a lot but the ball is already rolling on most of these projects.

I am not blind to the fact that the path is long and there will be hurdles and dips and drops along the way. There are a lot of things to do, but I have to start somewhere.

This is my plan to find Hippie Kushi (Hippie happiness) and this all became clear to me through meditation and a travel experience to an amazing place (you should try it).

Recognition

These sorts of experiences do change you though. Suddenly your friends, family and work colleagues see a change in you. You start to grow your hair long and your beard takes on a funky form. You start to dress differently and appear to have a new inner peace. I am obsessed with the Sadhus of India and I often dress like one; some friends from my former life think I've gone mad. For me, and I expect you, it's a wonderful transition, you are becoming who you want to be. You start visiting India – Goa especially and find yourself attracted to Eastern religion.

You scream out loud from the middle of a rainbow circle, "I'm happy!!!"

But everybody else says, "Oh dear, he's gone a bit weird, midlife crisis."

Colleagues have said to me, "You need a haircut, why are you growing your hair? You should trim your beard – it doesn't suit you."

What they really mean is it doesn't suit them! They hold their own conservative ideas and struggle to recognise this new you. But the most important thing is 'you' recognise you, you are happy with the new invigorated person you have become and if you lose friends along the way, you will make new ones in this new world (life) you have chosen.

I'm not saying that we should all become hippies of course. Perhaps once you have accepted the change in yourself, you may choose to become a biker, an artist, a writer, a rock star, a traveller or vagabonder – a member of a new age community, a Hare Krishna or even a naturist; don't let anyone steer you away from the path that makes you happy.

You have woken up to life!!! Embrace it, go with it and LIVE!!!

Chapter Three
Festivals, a Previously Undiscovered Joy!

Believe it or not, up until this point I had never been to a festival. So it was interesting that the very first thing I did after returning from my epiphany moment in Goa, was to attend my first ever festival. This is a perfect example of how I had lost my way as I got older. The fact that I had never gone to a festival before is quite sad and I had really missed out. Yes, I had gone to the gay pride party in the park and a few one-day concert events but I had never experienced the feeling of a five-day festival.

I had no idea of the love and friendship festivals could hold; the fun of camping out, meeting new people and dancing to live music to the early hours. My first festival was The Wilderness Festival.

Wilderness Festival UK

For those of you who are regular festival-goers, you know that feeling; it's as though you have entered a parallel universe but in the best possible way. Good festivals are places of togetherness, love, companionship and kindred spirits. Festivals are a place to meet people, to dance, to talk, to make new friends and to listen to some incredible music. Festivals are what the world could be. But up until the Wilderness festival, this particular stupid 'full stop' individual (yes, I'm talking about me) had never been to one. After I had experienced a good festival, there was no going back for me!

I ended up going to this particular festival by accident; my friend David announced out of the blue that he had bought tickets for the two of us and I needed to book the time off work. The UK was having a heatwave at the time and temperatures were very high during my five-day adventure into the Oxford countryside.

David drove us up from Hampton and even the journey was something to remember. We drove through areas of forest, beautiful old villages with thatched cottages and passed pretty medieval churches. We drove along tight country lanes and had to avoid tractors and people on horseback as we went.

The two of us were some of the first festival-goers to arrive at the site and we parked up quickly before struggling across fields to erect our tent. David, being a man of style and comfort, soon had the tent looking like a palace and before long our tent became part of a massive canvas town of festival-goers, and so we were ready to explore the Wilderness site.

But what is the Wilderness festival all about?

Adam Bloodworth of the Metro newspaper wrote this article:

"Wilderness festival, like Secret Garden Party and Standon Calling, is one of a relatively new legion of festivals, and one which has been designed with experiences in mind, rather than the relentless headliner-chasing you'd associate with something such as Reading & Leeds. Wilderness has a particularly verdant setting. Rather than pander to the programme, guests are more likely to be gently rolling out a much wider festival experience, where stirring countryside, lake swimming, and general daytime conviviality compete with high-energy nightlife from some of the most ambitious clubbing stages in the country. Wilderness is most similar to Latitude festival if it had to be likened to anything, because of its spectacularly verdant setting and multi-disciplinary line-up. But Wilderness does it better by integrating its thousands of acts with more of a natural sense of cohesion. It could be the lack of big-name acts that ultimately makes Wilderness as relaxing as it is because there are never big crowds to fight through – although the neatly formed queues for feasting tables give the cricket umpires a run for their money in the frightfully British stakes."

For me, my first impressions were of a huge crazy new age summer fair, full of funky looking freaks. One thing that should be pointed out is right from the beginning this was an eco-friendly event; paper straws, recycling bins, vegan food, bio-degradable cups and bottles and so on.

First of all, we walked down to the lake which is in a beautiful green setting, surrounded by forest and hills. The setting for this festival is breath-taking. As we neared the path up to the festival arena, we could see hot tubs and yurts in the distance with smoke billowing out of chimneys. This gave the impression of us approaching some kind of tribal village.

As we climbed the hill we stepped into a magical pagan setting of wigwams, tepees and yurts.

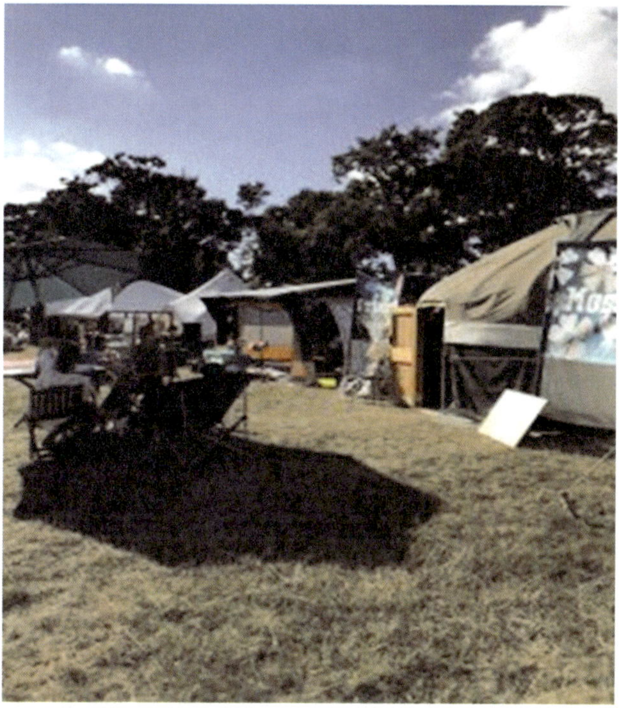

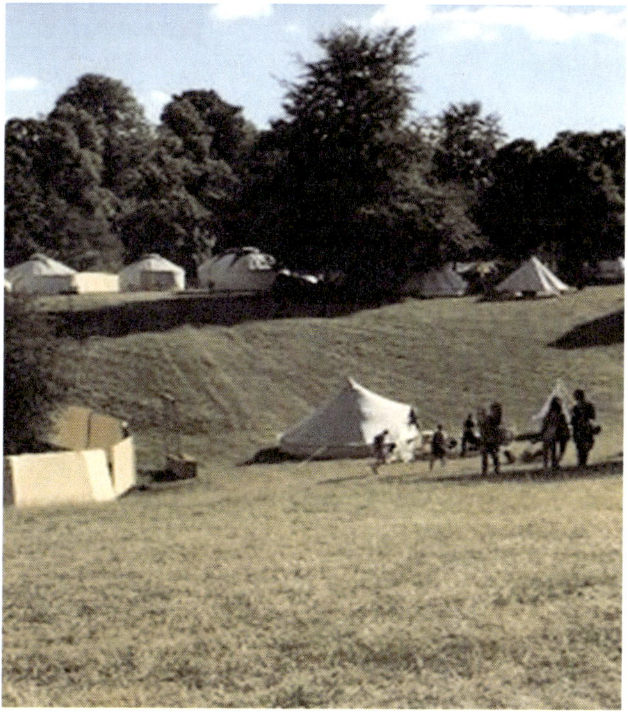

Dreadlocked and long-bearded new-agers were working on wooden spinning wheels making cloth while other tents had beautiful North African and Asian rugs laid out for sale. Strange statues, carvings and wicker furniture gave the whole area a kind of hippie community feel.

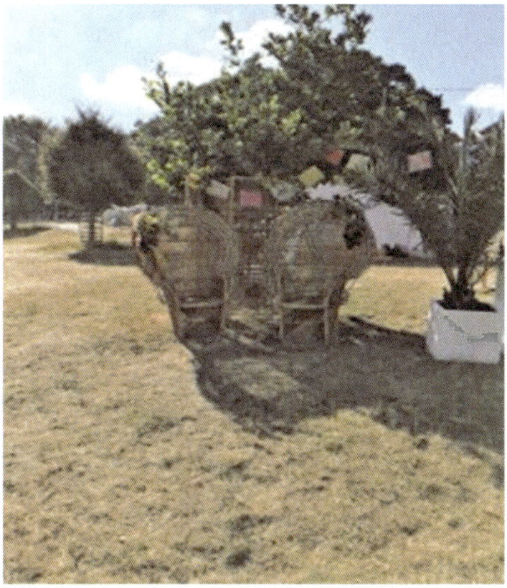
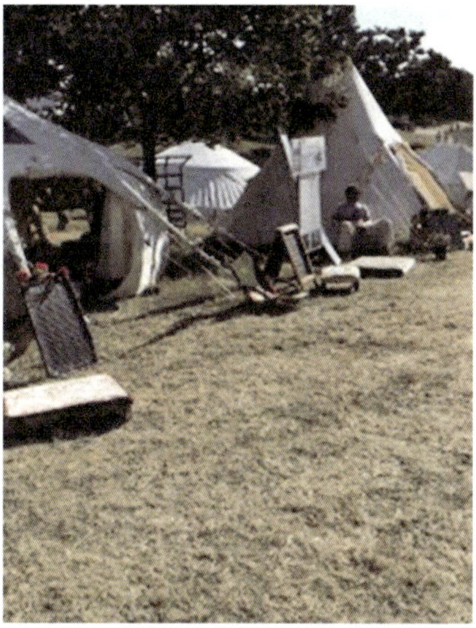
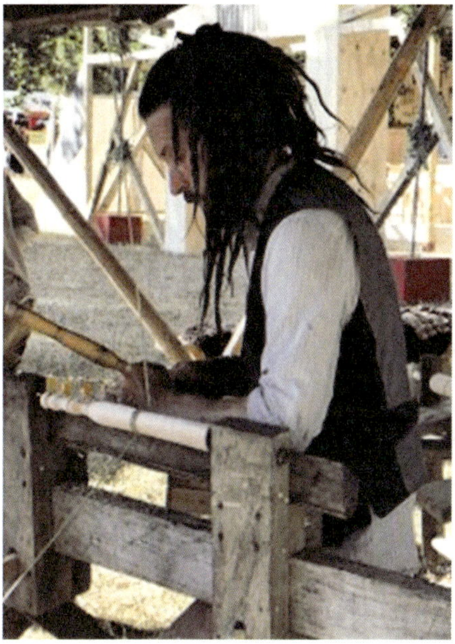
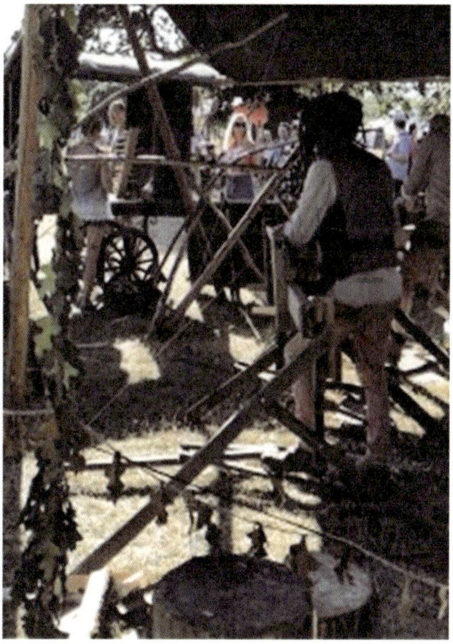

My first thoughts were that the festival was very quiet but this was silly as it was the first day and throughout that day more and more people arrived and the festival got busier and busier and the atmosphere began to change from quiet reflection to a buzz of anticipation.

When it came time to eat, the selection was vast. Every country in the world seemed to be represented here; Mexican, Cuban, Persian, Thai, Greek, Italian and Indian as well as plenty of vegan and vegetarian stalls.

This is when I realised this was not a cheap festival, prices are high (£12 burger, £6 a pint of beer), so bring plenty of cash. Lucky for us we stumbled upon a New York school bus/restaurant called The Bhangra Bus Cafe, selling delicious Thai based vegan food at as little as £6 a plate; needless to say, we returned there a few times.

After socialising back at our tent over a bottle of wine with other festival-goers, we set out for the evening's entertainment. The bars and clubs were in full swing, playing everything from psychedelic rock, reggae, jazz to trance, tribal and '80s disco. Was that weed I could smell (Surely not)?

The freaks were well and truly out to play. Seeing so many amazing looking people meant my camera was constantly on the go. We then came across the Atrium stage where I was introduced to a stunning band called 'My Baby'. I loved them so much I bought their album when I got back.

My Baby are a Dutch-New Zealand band from Amsterdam. Their music is a mix of blues, country, trance and funk.

At this festival there are two big stages, the main stage and the Atrium stage, as well as smaller stages such as the Travelling Barn where other music types can be heard; folk, classical, jazz, world music, country and western; basically, something for everyone.

The highlight of the festival for me was the people watching and the characters we sat and chatted to. We met some really cool and interesting people. We danced, we partied and we drank lots of cider.

Needless to say, we had sore heads the next day. So, after cooking breakfast on a camping stove we headed down to the lake. The whole five days were scorching hot and so people were jumping in the lake in their droves; some naked, others a little more conservative. With all the muscles around I thought I should join a gym when I got back.

David had a dip and enjoyed a swim in the deep cool waters but as I am still learning to swim, I stuck to sitting on the river bank enjoying the view.

We had a lot of fun at the cricket area, with festival-goers dressing up as famous characters and playing a comedy cricket game which featured no less than 80 streakers invading the pitch. The compare was very funny and it made a fun change from the noise of the clubs.

The highlight of the second night was to be found on the main stage. Chic and Nile Rogers played all their hits. Thousands came to watch the set regardless of whether this was their kind of music or not, and the atmosphere was electric, we danced the night away. I find at festivals it does not matter if you are a fan of a certain band or not – if you get into the atmosphere of the event, you will enjoy anything.

We were told that after this concert an all-night trance party was taking place in the valley. David wanted to go but this old hippie was ready for bed (this was before my return to Whirl-y-Gig, don't forget; how times have changed since then).

On the Sunday, the last official day of the festival, we had a more relaxing day and enjoyed just taking in the sights. The main act in the evening was Bastille and we joined the ever-growing crowd to watch. Halfway through the show, a group of amazing looking new-age hippies arrived. They were obviously all very close friends and they looked really cool in their weird outfits. I so wanted to know who they were but with the crowd all leaving the stage area after the show, we quickly lost them. When I think back to it now, the truth is I wanted to be those funky looking people. I wanted to live the life I imagined they were living. I wanted to dress like them, grow my hair like them and party like them. What I didn't realise at the time was psychologically I was already unconsciously on that path.

Monday morning meant it was time to leave and as we packed up our tent and left the site (with much difficulty due to the traffic making their way out) I had time to reflect on the festival.

I think my problem was that in the beginning I arrived with preconceptions of how a festival was going to be (based on never having been to one). Once I accepted this was something quite different to that, more of a funky new-age summer fayre, I relaxed and began to really enjoy it. In some instances, it felt like quite a middle-class festival, there are a lot of well-spoken beautiful people there but equally, there were plenty of others having a great time. For me, it was all about the people, not just the music. The characters we met made it the great experience it was. Wilderness festival gets a thumbs up from me.

After attending this festival and subsequently attending the Whirly Fayre, I now understand the importance of festivals and how they can leave you with a real sense of positivity and joy. I have the festival bug now and want to attend more and more of them. Festivals are an important part of waking up to life because they are how life should be; full of love, togetherness, creativity and joy. Festivals are about BEING ALIVE!!!

Other Great Festivals

WOMAD Festival:

WOMAD was founded in 1980 by English rock musician Peter Gabriel and friends. The first WOMAD festival was in Shepton Mallet, UK, in 1982. The audience saw Peter Gabriel, Don Cherry, The Beat, Drummers of Burundi, Echo & The Bunnymen, Imrat Khan, Prince Nico Mbarga, Simple Minds, Suns of Arqa, The Chieftains and Ekome amongst others performing.

Since 1982, WOMAD Festivals have travelled all over the world, bringing artists to numerous locations and entertaining over one million people. The main UK event was held at Rivermead in Reading, Berkshire, from 1990 until 2006.

In 2017 WOMAD UK marked its 35th anniversary. Headliners Emir Kusturica & The No Smoking Orchestra, Toots and The Maytals, Roy Ayers, Seun Kuti & Egypt 80 along with 30 other artists performed for a record-setting audience for the festival of 10,000 people.

Ethos:

From the outset, the WOMAD name has reflected the festival's idea; to be embracing but non-definitive, inspiring and outward-looking; and more than anything, enthusiastic about a world that has no boundaries in its ability to communicate through music and movement.

Programming:

WOMAD has always presented music that they felt to be of excellence, passion and individuality, regardless of musical genre or geographical origin. WOMAD encourages collaboration amongst the artists they invite to perform. The first WOMAD Festival in 1982 had Echo and the Bunnymen join forces with the Drummers of Burundi, and WOMAD Abu Dhabi 2010, saw a collaboration between Tinariwen, TV on the Radio members Kyp Malone and Tunde Adebimpe, Grammy-winning producer Ian Brennan (music producer, author), and the French Algerian Mehdi from Speed Caravan.

Workshops:

Adult workshops are taken by the musicians and will involve dance, musical instruments and discussions. Children's workshops involve painting, circus skills, graffiti, modelling, storytelling and more.

- Taste the World. Musicians cook a choice of dish from their home country in front of an audience.
- Global Market. The Global Market sells international food and wares.

Location:

WOMAD in the UK takes place in the grounds of Charlton Park, a stately home in Wiltshire.

Source: Wikipedia

Into the Wild:

"Come along to Into the Wild's amazing summer festival! Probably one of the best festival experiences in the UK. With sublime world music, over 100 workshops, talks, woodland theatre, choirs, cinema, delicious street food stalls, survival skills, archery, fire making, fascinating talks, yoga, foraging, drumming, storytelling, dancing, award-winning kids' area, dance, spoken word, wild games and so much more. Step out into beautiful nature and learn new skills, eat delicious food, meet new like-minded friends and embrace a new kind of festival! All workshops, camping and music included; just an hour from London, in amongst the beautiful meadows and enchanted forests of Sussex. Family-friendly with kids of every age, there's something for everyone at Into the Wild! www.in2wild.com" Source: Facebook

Noisily Festival:

"Set deep in the rolling hills of Leicestershire at the heart of rural England, Noisily Festival of Electronic Music and Arts lies in one of the most beautiful wooded valleys in the country. Totally contained amongst the trees creating a safe haven where hedonism and escapism can flourish and thrive, Noisily Festival 2019 will play host to some of the most exciting musical talent from the UK and abroad, along with a plethora of performance, innovative installations and mind-bending visual arts. You can expect to hear an extremely diverse collection of music; ranging from Bass, Glitch and Breaks, through House and Disco, via the Noisily mainstay of Progressive Techno, and not forgetting the Liquid Stage which has fast become the best outdoor psychedelic trance experience in the UK. Whilst rooted in the electronic music scenes Noisily is a holistic environment which feeds the mind, body and soul. It's a celebration of psychedelic art and culture in a society which is increasingly looking within for happiness and fulfilment, and away from material goods and money as the definition of success.

We have an amazing, receptive and intelligent community of people who we aim to mobilise through transformational experience and creative expression. By inspiring personal growth and social responsibility via the medium of art, music and healing, we hope to empower the individual to affect real positive change in the world."

https://noisilyfestival.com Source: Facebook

*

Chapter Four
Whirl-Y-Gig: The Other Life Changing Event in My Life

'For all of those who claim, "I never want to grow up," get out there and see the world. Seek out the unknown. Never let go of your sense of wonder. Then you'll stay young.'
From Heartbreak to the Hippie Trail – Kenneth Liss

A Unique and Historic Clubbing Experience; WHIRL-Y-GIG: The Early Years

Whirl-y-Gig has become something very important to me. I know I have said this before but it has literally changed my life. I have some amazing new friends, I have experienced new venues and parties and an incredible festival. Whirl-y-

Gig has really opened up my horizons. 'But it's just a club'; I hear you say. It is so, so much more than that, it is a way of life.

I first visited Whirl-y-Gig in the late 1980s with my dear friend Nick. We lived in the Seven Sisters area of North London at the time and had only recently moved to the capital.

Nick and I were definitely of a similar mind-set in those days and were searching for something a little different from the horrible Stock, Aitkin and Waterman disco music of that period. We had always had a more eclectic taste in music; artists like Nick Drake, Tom Waits and Fella Kuti are examples of some of the stuff we liked to listen to back then. Coming from Brighton, the capital of small venue live music, we had got into a lot of music from all over the world and we were searching for a nightclub that played a more grown-up, out-there kind of sound.

Even in those days I was a bit of a colourful character and wanted to go somewhere where I felt comfortable and could express myself. In the 1980s, before the internet really got going, we found out about events and places to go via Time Out magazine and one day whilst flicking through its pages, we came across Whirl-y-Gig and our lives were about to change.

"Whirl-Y-Gig is the longest-running world music dance club in London. It was set up by Ros Madden as an experiment of the Association of Humanistic Psychology in 1981; he passed it on to the capable hands of DJ Monkey Pilot four years later. Ros Madden died on October 20th 2011 in Luton. Monkey Pilot plays a wide range of music in the club, primarily world music/dance music fusions, but also many other genres. Whirl-Y-Gig is hailed as one of the central venues for people from London's alternative community.

Whirl-Y-Gig also appears at festivals, showing both live bands, which are mixed on the spot by DJ Monkey Pilot, or DJ sessions. They appear at such festivals as Beautiful Days, the Whitby Musicport Festival and the Sunrise Celebration. They have appeared at the short-lived Canterbury Fayre and also at Womad Reading. They run their own record label called Whirl-Y-Music and have organised their own festival, the Whirl-Y-Fayre, which first took place on August 2013, and has taken place every August since.

Whirl-Y-Gigs have featured artists such as Banco De Gaia, System 7, Dreadzone, Australasia, Eat Static, Loop Guru, Baka Beyond, Transglobal Underground, Another Green World and Kamel Nitrate." Source Wikipedia

So, you can imagine our joy at finding such a place. Our first experience was mind-blowing. The people there were all dressed like crazy new-age hippies and the music was from all over the world; everything from African drummers, Indian traditional music to British folk music. We danced all evening and I fell in love with the place.

We quickly met new people there and met up with our new friends each week. We also became friends with the organisers, Mary and Richard Sutcliffe as well as many of the staff. We started to meet all these new exciting people outside of the club at bars and gigs and had the odd Whirl-y-Gig party at our flat.

Mary, one of the organisers soon took me under her wing and offered me the role of balloon man. As I have said earlier in this book, one of the main events each week was at the end of the night's partying, a huge painted parachute was drawn over the crowd and everyone would then sit on the floor. Then, to ambient sounds and psychedelic lighting, balloons would tumble onto the parachute creating a magical and mystical experience.

As previously stated, my job, for a princely sum of £10, was to blow up the balloons and distribute them to the crowd prior to the parachute descending. The parachute moment still takes place at the club today.

There used to be someone at the door of the club who did face painting and as part of my persona, I had my face painted every week and became famous in the club as the balloon man.

When I arrived, people at the club would say, "Hey, it's the Balloon Man!"

Of course, I loved it and played my role well.

A Melting Pot of Creativity

"The regular crowd of Whirly-giggers are warm and welcoming and the stewarding is professional, friendly and caring. From the moment you walk through the doors through to the legendary parachute that culminates the night, Whirl-Y-Gig is a bubble of positivity and a melting pot of creativity where one can escape the burdens and prejudices of day-to-day life. Whirl-Y-Gig is an event difficult to describe and a moment difficult to miss. With a strong and loving life force, the Whirl-Y-Sound is a musical heartbeat for a future global family. The intense atmosphere, the diverse clientele, that constant intimacy and openness – this is the way that Whirl-y-Gig has been since its inception in the 1980s." Source: www.vice.com

Whirl-y-gig is still going 38 years later.

We both stopped going as we got older, that was over 30 years ago and a lot has changed since then in my life, as the pages of this book have explained. Whirl-y-Gig became a distant happy memory.

A Trip on the Whirl-Y-Gig Time Machine

Years later I was sitting in a pub in the West End reminiscing with my dear friend, Nick; the friend I used to go with all those years ago. We had gotten on to the subject of Whirl-y-Gig and how I was thinking of going back to see what it was like all these years later. You see, Nick and I would attend Whirl-y-Gig religiously every week at the end of the 1980s to the mid-1990s. We made many good friends in those days and it held a lot of fond memories for us.

The trance and dance music played at Whirl-y-Gig today is really fantastic but in the 1990s it had a slightly different flavour and although the 'world music' theme still ran through it, we danced to a different beat back then; but those same happy feelings still rang true.

One of my earliest memories of Whirl-y-Gig is hearing the Penguin Cafe Orchestra. I went out and bought their album immediately afterwards.

Another fond memory was the Gypsy Kings.

Transglobal Underground was a real triumph; as well as Afro Celt Sound System. I'm still a huge fan of Transglobal Underground today.

Here are just some examples of tracks played at that time and these are only the ones beginning with the letter A:

Source: www.discogs.com

Acorn Arts – Silence 12″ [1992] – progressive house/trance with an uplifting piano riff.

Adiemus – Kayama [1995]

African Business – In Zaire (Maria Mix) 12″ [1990]

Afro Celt Sound System – Whirl-y-Reel CDS [1996]

Age of Love – Age of Love (Watch Out for the Stella Mix) CDS [1992] – a trance classic

Ali Farka Toure & Ry Cooder – Amandrai CD: Talking Timbuktu [1994] – downtempo track

Angélique Kidjo – Adouma (12" Mix) CDS [1994] – remixed by The Shamen

Another Green World – Pilots mirror [1996] – this was a classic parachute track, released earlier on one of their cassette albums.

Antico – We Need Freedom 12" [1991]

Apache Indian – Move Over India / Come Follow Me CD: No Reservations [1993]

Art of Trance – Cambodia 12" [1994]

Astralasia – Celestial Ocean 12" [1991]

Astralasia – Unveria Zekt CDS [1993] – (Kobian Love Chant mix)

And so, after all these years, I bought a ticket to attend Whirl-y-Gig for its next outing in London on December 2018. I was really looking forward to returning to that amazing place and seeing how I felt about it, all these years later. Little did I know how much it would change my life and add to the hippie Kushi person I was becoming.

*

Whirl-Y-Gig, My Return

I felt like a child at Christmas when I woke up in Hampton on a misty winter's morning, it was Saturday, December 8th, Whirl-y-Gig day!!!

I was returning to Whirl-y-Gig for the first time in well over thirty years. In fact, it would be the first time I had been clubbing for about 20 years and so it was wonderful that it was Whirl-y-Gig that was to be my first in so long. But would it be the same? Would the love and togetherness still be there? Would I be the only oldie in a club full of kids? Only one way to find out – I had my ticket and my outfit was on the hanger.

First of all, I wanted to get ready the old way, with a bottle of wine and some pumping music in my flat. By the time I was ready to make the journey I was deep in the Whirly mood and up for a party.

Luckily, I had my headphones on and my tribal beats banging in my ears as I made the hour and a half journey to Bow Road in London on the underground. As I had arrived a bit early, I popped into a local East End pub for a pint. It felt a bit rough as I entered; everyone went quiet and looked over at the stranger in the hippie garb. It was like a scene out of the Wild West, only no gunslingers, just an alien from planet Whirl-y-Gig. They then just carried on their business and I relaxed with a pint; the freaks were in town tonight.

Me and Geoff; someone I met on that first night and who has now become a good friend.

I then made the short walk to the Bloc nightclub; there was already a small queue of eager clubbers. Straight away I felt that family feeling, people welcomed me with enthusiasm and some recognised me from my blog. I was made immediately welcome and after looking at the people in the queue I answered my first question; it was clearly a multicultural and mixed age group event, just like the old days.

As the queue got larger it was surely going to be a packed club in there. We were soon ushered to the door to make our entry. This bit surprised me, the security checks were more like airport customs, with full bag checks, pat-downs and even my wallet was searched. This was very different from the last time I came to whirly; I guess it's a sign of the times, a lot has happened in the world since 1990.

Once I entered the club, I got a good idea of the layout. The café selling cakes, fruit, coffee and tea was still there; just like before. The cloakroom staff were warm and friendly as I put in my bag for the night. This initial area had tables and chairs and doubled up as the club's chill-out area.

I then passed through some double doors to a sort of corridor area. To the right were alcoves with leather sofas – a nice place to chat and meet new people. The ceiling in this corridor was very low and it felt a little claustrophobic. To the left was the bar, I went over and ordered a can of red stripe (no draft) – the beer was £5 – a bit of a shock but the club has to make money somehow.

I stood at the bar a while and within ten minutes multiple people had come over, greeted me and introduced themselves. I felt it then, that Whirl-y-Gig family feeling, that love and companionship, it was still there and I smiled; I'm back. All these people were dressed in colourful clothes, with crazy hats and beads; I love the freaky people.

I then entered the dance floor and was elated to see the familiar set up – giant balloons floated around the room, coloured lights illuminated the painted material draped all around and huge globes hung from the ceiling; oh, to be back with an old friend.

Then I saw Richard, aka Monkey Pilot, on the decks, wearing his famous hat.

I walked onto the stage to greet him but before I reached him, he opened his arms and shouted, "Stephen!"

We hugged and reminisced – it was beautiful. The crazy thing is, he hasn't aged a day in 30 years, a bit greyer around the gills but just the same – the man is some sort of alien immortal god and his natural warmth oozed out of every pour.

It didn't take long for the club to become very, very busy and the atmosphere was incredible. Monkey Pilot played a mix of musical styles on the decks: global dance, tribal, reggae, house, trance, Goa psytrance and jazz fusion.

I met so many wonderful characters and they made me feel like I belonged there – I was now back in the fold. One great example of the many chameleons I met was Geoff who has been coming to Whirl-y-Gig for many, many years and is also a regular Goa, India visitor. He is proof that you are never too old to embrace life and party!!!

Geoff

Another important person from my past Whirly days was eluding me at this point but I finally stumbled upon Mary (Whirl-y-Gig's co-runner and host) in the chill-out area chatting to someone. I said hi and she recognised me straight away. She was a little busy but we exchanged a few words and she suggested that, as it has been so many years since I was last the Whirl-y-Gig balloon man, that I might like to blow up a few balloons before the parachute event later in the proceedings. I thought this was a lovely idea and was really thoughtful. I said that after not clubbing for so many years I might not make it to 5:30 a.m. but I would give it a good go. Mary, too, had not aged a day since 1990; I want some of what they're having.

The evening was a wild one, and although I was very much still there at 5:30 a.m. I think we were both caught up in the evening and I didn't get around to blowing up those balloons (next time Mary). She sent me a lovely message after that night that said:

'Good to see you at Whirly on Saturday, hopefully, see you there again when we can get time to chat and introduce you to the crew, have a good month, dear one.'

Mary and Richard, you are the 'dear ones' – Beautiful faeries and immortals.

Later on, I met a group of lovely young people and one of them, Ben, came and sat next to me for a chat. After meeting and chatting to all his mates, we all made friends and I ended up spending much of the evening with them.

For the rest of the night, I danced and danced. I haven't danced like that for years. I didn't feel like an oldie – I felt invigorated and alive. I knew then that I would embrace this world.

I met so many wonderful people that night and I knew when I came again to Whirl-y-Gig we would greet each other with warmth as new friends and I knew that many of those amazing crazy souls would become my friends outside of Whirl-y-Gig too. I cannot really explain what I mean by the Whirly feeling but it is a kind of kinship, togetherness and a feeling of love. We hugged, we embraced and we danced the night away.

By the time the parachute was pulled out over us and we all sat on the floor for the chill moment, I felt warm inside. I felt loved and I felt like I belonged.

It was a wonderful moment to recognise that Whirl-y-Gig is alive and kicking. It is unique and truly the best club in the world!!!

I have returned to Whirl-y-Gig time and again since that night. I was right about the friends I made there too; we have all become very close and I feel being a Whirly regular is like being part of a unique tribe, a family; I love it. And Nick, if you are reading this, why don't you come along for the ride sometime as well…

Nick in 2019

*

Chapter Five
Why Whirl-Y-Gig Continues to Be So Important in My Life

You may be asking at this point, 'But why would going to a nightclub be a life-changing experience?'

Because, Whirl-y-Gig is no ordinary nightclub – it's more of a creative melting pot.

Another event, Parlour Party is a perfect example of this melting pot.

Parlour Party is a separate project of Mary and Richard Sutcliffe's (the Whirl-y-Gig organisers and hosts/DJ), but very much linked into the Whirly vibe. It's an audience participation open mic night with a creative, arty, joyful and folksy feel. Many of the Whirl-y-Gig regulars attend this event and get up and perform music and poetry there and their range of talent is mind blowing.

This explosion of artistic talent sums up what the appeal of Whirl-y-Gig is; it's full of fantastic artistic, creative people of all ages.

Someone with this creative verve is Geoff Sarbutt (the writer of one of the forwards to this book). He was the first person I ever really got to know at Whirl-y-Gig (pictured far left of the photo above). Through my many conversations with Geoff, I found out he used to live on a canal boat, something I aspire to do in the near future. Geoff also loves to travel and takes himself off to Europe on a regular basis, as do I. So, there was instantly a connection when I met him. I now enjoy meeting up with Geoff on a regular basis to enjoy a beer or a gig now and again – we especially like a boat pub moored between Vauxhall and Lambeth bridges in London, where we talk about life, the universe and everything in-between. It turns out Geoff spends a few months every year living in Goa. His favourite place in Goa is Benaulim in the South of that wonderful Indian state. Benaulim still has that laid back hippie vibe but it's a lot quieter than places like Anjuna or Arambol in the North.

I have returned to Goa on several occasions since that first fateful trip few years back. This January, I am spending four wonderful weeks in Goa and the first week I will be spending with Geoff in Benaulim.

This is what I mean about Whirl-y-Gig and the connections you make – from that first encounter with Geoff I now have a good friend that I meet up with regularly to go out for a pint, someone to enjoy Parlour Party with and also now to spend time with in India.

More examples of these wonderful Whirl-y-Gig connections are the rest of my new crew: Louise, Las and James.

Las (pictured second right) initially gravitated towards me – he loves to dance and had seen me strutting my stuff on the dance floor on my second visit to Whirly. He introduced himself to me and every time after that we would sit together, chat and later dance the night away together. I realised pretty quickly that this was a special guy – his warmth and gentle soul shines through. Since then, Las and I have been to places such as Club Psymera and Tribal Village together – he came to my Whirly party at my flat and recently he came for his first visit to Parlour Party which he loved and now attends each month. He has become a good friend and I can safely say he is one of the nicest and most sincere people I have ever met. He is now planning on joining me and the rest of our crew in Goa next year.

James (first right in the photo) came over and spoke to me at Whirly from day one; he is an enthusiastic Whirly regular and quite knowledgeable about the club's history. Our initial conversations were short and I did not really get to know him well at the beginning but when I was looking for a volunteer to drive me to the Whirly Fayre festival in Somerset, James instantly volunteered even though he lived quite far from me. I thought this was a lovely gesture and on that long journey to the festival, I finally got to know him better and we bonded and became friends. Since then, as well as our regular visits to Whirl-y-Gig, James has accompanied me to Parlour Party on a few occasions now.

Now, let's talk about Louise (centre of the photo looking her normal mischievous self). I was initially introduced to Louise and her friend Melissa on my first outing to Whirly – I knew straight away they were a nice fun couple of young ladies (I say young… cough… lol). I think Louise wasn't too sure about me at first but as time went by, she got to know me better and we began to bond. It turned out that as well as Las (who lives in Surrey), Louise lived not too far from me as well, in Surbiton.

When I had my Whirl-y-Gig/Hippie Kushi house party in Hampton last summer, she came over and it really started to feel like we were becoming good friends and soon after she had me and Las over for dinner.

It was at the Whirly Fayre though that we all became proper family. After my tent was destroyed by the first night storm (more about that later), Louise lent me her spare tent and we pitched up next to each other. We all had such a lovely time at the festival but Louise and I were the ones who really connected and I think of her now as one of my best friends. Since the fayre we have attended several clubs together. She has invited me on a few occasions to her favourite local bar in Surbiton, called the Blue Orchid, where I have met more new lovely people and Louise is also going to Goa at the same time – I will be there in February 2020.

All of these new and exciting friends have led to me experiencing new clubs and events, meeting even more new people and enjoying the love and support you get from a group of wonderful close friends.

My point is, if I was still sitting at home every weekend watching TV, none of these connections would have happened.

'You have to get out there, be brave and come out of your comfort zone in order to experience the new and exciting.'

Through Whirl-y-Gig, my life has gotten so much more interesting, much more social and remains full of love and friendship to this day.

Back in August 2019, these new friendships would soon lead to something that will stay with me for the rest of my life. After some gentle persuasion, I was talked into attending a four-day event in the rolling hills of Somerset. Everyone had been raving about it for months. Little did I know at that time what to expect when I purchased my ticket. What awaited me was a kaleidoscope of feelings, a fantastic cacophony of kinship, creativity, positivity, togetherness and love. This explosion of artistic flamboyance in Somerset was the magnificent Whirly Fayre!

*

Chapter Six
Whirl-Y-Fayre

"Walking Among the Spirits and Dancing with Fairies in the Vale of Avalon"

I can honestly say I was 100% a changed man after attending this festival; my whole outlook changed and I felt I could achieve anything I wanted, my dreams were within reach. I had been told how wonderful it was, how the people were, about the hippie vibe, the love, the kinship; but I never expected the emotional affect it had on me.

Everybody at the Fayre was living a hippie Kushi life, they looked amazing and I felt we could really change the world. I cannot recommend the Whirl-y-Fayre more. If you go you will embrace the community as I have.

I have struggled with how to word this chapter, how to capture that feeling, the way it made me feel; so I have decided to do it with the help of a few famous hippie quotes, to sum up that emotion, that feeling of elation that I felt.

Whirly Fayre:

"The whirl-y-fayre is a gathering of kindred spirits in beautiful and mystical AVALON. Lasting images of the Fayre are the smiling faces of whirly folk, children, adults, young people, all free from life's cares, and enjoying each other's company amidst colourful whirly environments and lovely green meadows. Many liken it to faery land with circus tents, pretty bunting and cosmic decor, delicious meals and homemade cakes and smoky crackling fires. Night-time lights twinkle and blaze with exotic colours, turning the whole of whirl-y-land into a faery dream, and one which no one wants to wake from. Meanwhile, the whirly artists are on a quest. They live to do so much more than simply entertain. They excel at bringing joy. They transport us to that realm beyond imagination, a realm which makes us want to dance ourselves alive, to be here now, and to know that everything is worth it! The whirl-y-fayre leaves a warm afterglow which goes on and on. Deep in the heart of Avalon, it connects us with our childlike innocence, and a newfound confidence, no matter what else has happened in our lives. It unlocks an energy which stays until the next fayre, leaving us moving forward with joy, spirits lifted and just so excited to have something so brilliant to look forward to!" www.whirl-y-fayre.co.uk

"I walked among the spirits and danced with fairies in the Vale of Avalon. I have never felt more of a connection to Gaia than I did during this festival.
Thank you for the memories, thank you for allowing us into your sacred spaces to heal. Thank you EVERY SINGLE person at Whirly fayre for your warmth and compassion and hugs.
Your Vibe attracts your tribe."
Danny Payne
On Facebook

As the sun came up over Stonehenge, the Fairies, hippies and mystical people made their way to the Vale of Avalon.

"Never doubt that a small group of thoughtful, committed individuals can change the world, indeed it's the only thing that ever has." — Margaret Meade

"Imagine no possessions, I wonder if you can. No need for greed or hunger. A brotherhood of man. Imagine all the people sharing all the world." — *John Lennon*

I stood in the stairwell of my flat's block in Hampton, looking out of the window, waiting eagerly for my friend James from Whirl-y-Gig to arrive to drive me to Somerset for the festival. I couldn't thank him enough for offering to pick me up, especially as he lived quite far from me. It was Thursday, August 15th 2019, and an event I had been excited about for ages had finally arrived.

I felt like a child at Christmas when James drove into my drive. I pulled my camping trolley over to his car – it was full of bags of colourful outfits, a tent, a stove, a cool box full of booze and my bedding, ready for the four-day event.

"Love is a friendship set to music." — Joseph Campbell

The drive was quite long but the scenery was beautiful; rolling hills, full of greenery and livestock. We stopped off at a pretty country pub on the way and the food there was lovely. Once we had filled our bellies, we were ready for the last leg of the trip; we only hoped we could find the site. The fayre was quite near to Glastonbury set amongst the beautiful countryside in Somerset.

After getting a little bit lost driving up several country lanes, we suddenly found ourselves at the fayre; we had arrived and my head exploded with expectation.

Geoff, who had arrived a couple of hours before us, had decided on a spot in the middle of the field just up the hill from the main dance tent. The wind was up and it turned into a nightmare trying to put up my tent. The tent's design was flawed and it kept collapsing. I had concerns for that first night as the weather forecast was for strong winds and rain.

Little did we know what was to come…

I don't want to dwell on this as the Fayre was truly amazing but that first night and the next day the weather was horrendous; gale-force winds and rain.

My tent collapsed during the night and I knew I could not remain in it for the rest of the fayre. Luckily my friend Louise had a spare and I was able to move to that one, next to her tent; which turned into a nice arrangement. We created our own little compound and this set up allowed us to really get to know each other and we created a little whirly family compound.

Me, James, Louise and our new friend: Richard the leprechaun.
"To plant a garden is to believe in tomorrow." — Audrey Hepburn

The people began to arrive, and oh the people. Fantastic colourful hippies, painted freaks, leather-clad Gothic circus people, and many, many wonderful whirly people; it was going to be something special. The warmth of the welcome, the hugs, the kinship, the love; we were ready for that first night party.

"To live a creative life, we must lose our fear of being wrong." — Joseph Chilton Pearce

The welcome party on that first night was amazing. After a warm welcome from Richard and Mary; our lovely, lovely hosts, we found to our surprise there was a free 'help yourself' bar. The DJ, Chris (JungleChris) Woolvett, played a brilliant Drum n Bass/ Jungle set and this was when I realised I really liked this kind of music.

Everyone was dancing and going crazy to this amazing vibe. We met up with loads of our regular whirly friends and met a few new ones too.

"To be beautiful means to be yourself. You don't need to be accepted by others. You need to accept yourself." — Thich Nhat Hanh

This is when I first met Danny and his friends. They walked into the party like a tornado, colourful walking canes (staffs) in their hands, dressed like new-age global nomads; they lit up the room. I was immediately attracted to this group and Danny's aura and positive energy made me smile. I soon started up a conversation with him.

We spent much of the fayre enjoying the company of these guys and Danny in-particular caught my attention because of his warm, gentle heart and inquisitive mind and personality.

I hoped we would be friends after this fayre – I loved dancing with those crazy guys; they really had an effect on me.

Danny sent me a lovely message after the fayre saying how much he had enjoyed the fayre and meeting us all.

I heard he enjoyed the Fayre so much that he bought a ticket for the 'Into the Woods' festival the following weekend; such staying power.

"Life is short. Don't waste it being sad. Be who you are, be happy, be free, be whatever you want to be." — Unknown

Many of my photos from this weekend are quite blurry and strange. That's because most of the time I was totally off my fucking tits!!! I really went for it big style. We gotta let our hair down some times. And I quite like the photographic results. We will discuss Sex, drink, drugs, and rock n roll in a later chapter.

"My business is to enjoy and have fun. And why not, if in the end, everything will end, right?" — Janis Joplin

Paul and Gerry; gods amongst men

    This is Paul and Gerry; we know them from Whirl-y-Gig and were so happy they attended the fayre. They are totally crazy and totally lovely and gorgeous guys. We call them The Cornish Farmers because Paul looks like one (right of picture) and they both live in Cornwall (OK, what do you want, Freudian analysis?). They had a nice set up on the campsite; two campervans together with a tent in the middle. We slipped over to their compound for a party on the Sunday afternoon, it was naughty but nice!

"Love is all you need." — The Beatles

Louise and Mellissa

After the rain stopped on Friday afternoon, the sun came out and the event really took off. My group of friends and I made our way down to the main tent.

Monkey Pilot and some great guest bands played some fantastic music: Drum n Bass, Psytrance and world music. We danced the night away. There were so many people to say hello to and loads of new friends to meet. The crowd was colourful and crazy; I went to bed smiling.

"I do my thing, and you do your thing. I am not in this world to live up to your expectations, and you are not in this world to live up to mine. You are you, and I am I, and if by chance we find each other, it's beautiful." — Frederick E. Perl

"Do you want me to tell you something really subversive? Love is everything it's cracked up to be. That's why people are so cynical about it. It really is worth fighting for, being brave for, risking everything for. And the trouble is, if you don't risk anything, you risk even more." — Erica Jong

During the day we chilled out, listened to our music on portable speakers and visited our friends as well as making new ones; it was beautiful. At two p.m. Parlour Party (Whirl-y-Fayre version) would start and people would get up and perform on the open mic stage. The talent was incredible and it was a nice gentle start to the craziness of the evening. After this, we would normally go for a wander around the site before getting tarted up back at our tents and have a few pre-party beers.

"My advice to people today is as follows: If you take the game of life seriously, if you take your nervous system seriously, if you take your sense organs seriously, if you take the energy process seriously, you must turn on, tune in, and drop out." — Timothy Leary

The setup of the site was as follows:

The Fayre sat comfortably on a hill in the beautiful rolling meadows and countryside of Somerset.

Up the hill in the centre and to the left were mainly tents and this felt like a wonderful colourful hippie community.

Up the top of the hill and down the right-hand side were the caravans, wigwams, motor homes and campervans. It was a wonderful nomadic hippie gipsy nirvana.

At the bottom of the left-hand side was the staff and volunteer camp and office caravan; a very busy area. And towards the bottom of the right-hand side, where the hill flattened out, were tepees and fire-pits. This area offered massage, Tai chi and other therapies and any support people required.

In the centre at the bottom were more fire pits, a lit-up fountain, a huge tree with lights and straw bales to sit on, a clothes shop, a pizza stall and a burger van. Here, there was also an amazing psychedelic art gallery tent which doubled up as a chill-out zone.

"Nobody living can ever stop me. As I go walking my freedom highway. Nobody living can make me turn back. This land was made for you and me." — Woody Guthrie

Then there were the two main tents; the restaurant tent serving breakfast lunch and dinner (vegetarian) very good and at a nice price. This place also housed the bar.

The biggest tent was the main dance floor and stage for the live music and DJ Monkey Pilot.

"You create your own reality." — *Seth*

After our pre-party at our compound, we all marched down the hill to the main tent for the night's shenanigans. Monkey Pilot (aka Richard Sutcliffe) took his place as Whirl-y-Gig's famous DJ to rapturous applause – his music has inspired me for many years – my early record collection was inspired by Richard: The Gypsy Kings, Penguin Cafe Orchestra and of course my favourite Transglobal Underground (who after all these years were performing at this very fayre). And now all these years since my first visit to Whirl-y-Gig my music collection is almost completely based on the fantastic music Monkey Pilot plays. You will always be a hero to me Richard and don't ever think otherwise. Needless to say, his sets throughout this Fayre were mind-blowing. Monkey Pilot was then joined on the stage by many guest live bands.

The bands were also amazing and we all danced like crazy people through the night; the room was full of joy. The highlights of the night for me were the wonderful people, the incredible music and dancing and seeing my legends: Transglobal Underground!!!

I danced all through their amazing set and was soaked through with sweat afterwards – they were awesome. When I stepped out of the main tent to cool down, I was met with a scene of wonder. There were fire dancers, people on stilts, crazy circus performers, a long dragon train and hippies dancing all around under a blood-red moon.

"With freedom, books, flowers, and the moon, who could not be happy?" — Oscar Wilde

During the day time we socialised, visiting other tents and campervans, we drank, laughed partied and boogied. It's really hard to put into words just how amazing Whirl-y-fayre was, so I will just have to do it with pictures:

Lovely Danny

"If you smile at me, I will understand because that is something everyone, everywhere does in the same language." — Jefferson Airplane

Me with some of my lovely new friends

"Old hippies don't die, they just lie low until the laughter stops and their time comes round again." — Joseph Gallivan

"If someone thinks love and peace is a cliché that must have been left behind in the '60s, that's his problem. Love and peace are eternal." — John Lennon

The famous Whir-y-Gig parachute finale
"Your mind is like a parachute, it doesn't work unless it's open." — Jordan Maxwell

As with Whirl-y-Gig the whole event wound up with the unravelling of the famous parachute; it seemed even more beautiful under the main tent canvas after such a lovely festival.

"You have to forget about what other people say, when you're supposed to die, or when you're supposed to be loving. You have to forget about all these things. You have to go on and be crazy. Craziness is like heaven." — Jimi Hendrix

Me and Geoff

"Follow your bliss and the universe will open doors where there were only walls." — Joseph Campbell

"The only people for me are the mad ones, the ones who are mad to live, mad to talk, mad to be saved, desirous of everything at the same time, the ones who never yawn or say a commonplace thing, but burn, burn, burn, like fabulous yellow roman candles exploding like spiders across the stars." — Jack Kerouac

"Go confidently in the direction of your dreams, Live the life you've always imagined." — Henry David Thoreau

I always knew I loved the outdoor life – I love camping and being amongst nature. At this fayre I met people who lived on the road, living in campervans fulltime and travelling from hippie community to hippie community. These conversations stimulated me so much. To live this sort of lifestyle calls out to me and I think it was these characters that I talked to at this incredible fayre that really left me a changed man.

> **"I'd rather wear flowers in my hair than diamonds around my neck. I don't want to earn a living, I want to live." — Oscar Wilde**

Readers who have been following my blog (hippiekushiwakinguptolife.com) for some time, know I have been in search of happiness and an alternative lifestyle; the lifestyle I was always meant to live. I was somebody who never fitted with the everyday.

Mike Hudson, in his book, 'How to live in a Van and Travel', summed up that feeling perfectly for me.

"Three years ago, I would sit at my desk every day and think 'this can't be it'. Nothing seemed to make sense. I felt like I was missing out, like there was so much more to life than going back and forth to an office building every day, feeling tired and unfulfilled. I needed to escape. I wanted to explore the world, live in different places, meet different people and let every day be an adventure. I wanted the life I thought might be out there. And if it didn't exist; I'd create it."

> **"The free soul is rare, but you know it when you see it – basically because you feel good, very good when you are near or with them."**
>
> *— Charles Bukowski*

I used Danny Payne's quote at the beginning of this chapter. It is clear from talking to him that this festival had a profound effect on him. I can safely say I too was deeply affected by the Whirly Fayre – the atmosphere was very stimulating. I came away knowing who I was and the kind of person I want to be. I adored the hippie atmosphere, the nomadic lifestyle, and the colourful people living alternative lifestyles. I was never made for a nine to five normal life. I was never made for four walls a garden and a mortgage. I want to travel. I want to live in a campervan or canal boat. I want to be free and I want to look the way I want to look. I want to have like-minded hippie friends. I want to be hippie Kushi.

Whirly Fayre stimulated all of this in me and made me feel MAGNIFICENT!!!

"If a man does not keep pace with his companions, perhaps it is because he hears the beat of a different drummer. Let him step to the music he hears, however measured or far away." — Henry David Thoreau

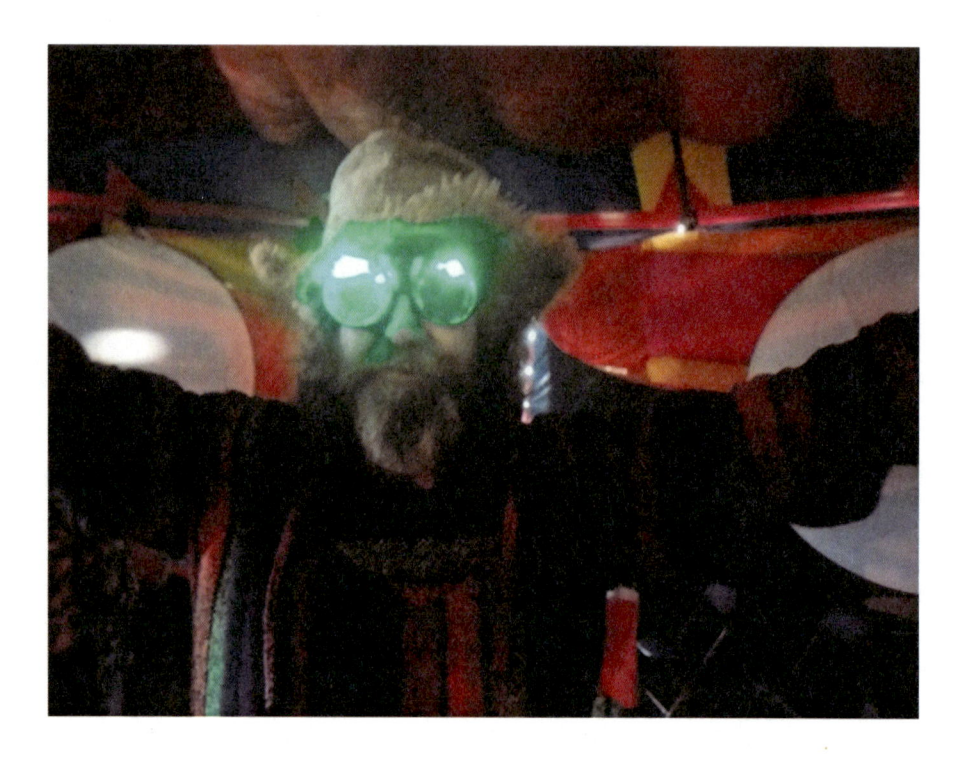

"Down through all of eternity the crying of humanity, this' then when the hurdy-gurdy man comes singing songs of love." — Donovan

Thank you, Mary, Richard and the team, the staff and all the volunteers for an amazing, life-affirming, life-changing event. I really cannot thank you enough for all your hard work and I am 1000,000% going to be back next year!!!

Mary Sutcliffe
(Whirl-y-Gig host and Fayre organiser and gorgeous faerie queen)

"I've been smiling lately, dreaming about the world as one. And I believe it could be. Someday it's going to come." — Cat Stevens

*

Chapter Seven
Grey Life, Grey World?

"Nothing Bad Ever Lasts"

But why are things like festivals and all this hippie stuff so important? Why should we embrace our hippie side and change our lives and the world? Why is it important to offer greater love, tolerance and togetherness to each other?

The answer is simple because our world began the process of becoming a darker, right-wing and more intolerant place when those planes crashed into the twin towers in New York in 2001.

18 years after 9/11 the world is changing before my eyes and not for the good. Every terrible thing I see makes me weep inside. History has shown us that sometimes things need to get really bad before they can get better again. Would it then be too late or would the cycle of ages begin again?

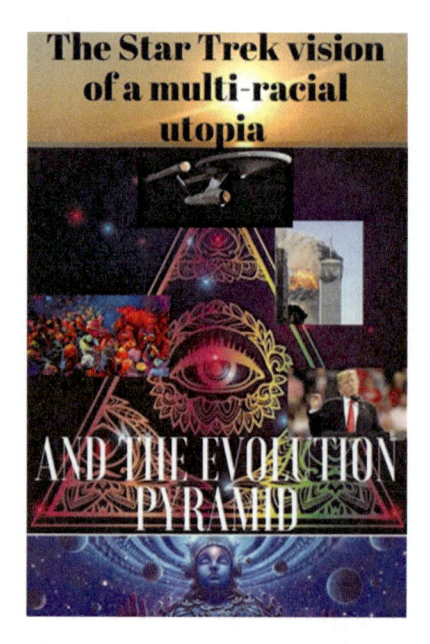

The Star Trek Vision of a Multi-Racial Utopia vs the Evolution Pyramid

This is a tricky subject for me and one that you may not all agree with and some might ask what it has to do with a search for happiness. The fact is the UK Brexit vote was, without a doubt, the worst day of my life. I am writing this on the morning after over 900,000 people marched through the streets of London protesting against Brexit. Let alone the thousands of extinction Rebellion protesters building their barriers to open up the world's eyes to the crisis our sick world is facing.

I know there are those in the world with hate in their hearts and they will always stand as a hurdle to a better collective ideal of togetherness, but equally, I have always believed that we human beings should all come together as 'one'. No one should have the right to tell you where you should live on this beautiful planet and if we could only try to understand each other a little better we might just make this world a better place.

So, where has it all gone wrong?

As a science fiction fan, I often think about the Star Trek vision of the future, where all nations, cultures and species of the world live together in harmony in a collective utopia. In this future utopia, the planet has been saved from global warming and cut free from humanities worst and most destructive habits.

Dave Schilling wrote about this vision in his article for the **Observer newspaper** called: **Star Trek's 50-year mission: to shine a light on the best of humankind**

"The visionary sci-fi series first aired in September 1966 – and its utopian, confident blueprint for society still resonates in the age of Trump."

"There is no grand political statement in the first episode of Star Trek, 50 years ago. The Man Trap is a languid little thriller about a monster that eats salt and has a curious habit of shape-shifting into the image of your ex-girlfriend.

"If you happened to tune in on September 8th 1966, you would have had no concept of the utopian idealism favoured by Star Trek's creator, Gene Roddenberry, no inkling of the socialist concepts of the sharing of resources that would pop up in later incarnations of the franchise. It was high adventure set in space, nothing more.

"But there's no question that what defines Star Trek today is an egalitarian, pluralistic, moral future society that has rejected greed and hate for the far more noble purpose of learning all that is learnable and spreading freedom throughout the galaxy."

Star Trek hoped for a future of tolerance and understanding but in reality, the evolution of humankind has instead taken a different path; a kind of evolution pyramid that was initially rising beautifully in the direction of the Star Trek dream that creator Gene Roddenberry believed possible; a dream where countries would come together as one and work as a collective for the greater good.

Before the year 2000, we in the UK were happily part of Europe; we were Europeans – not just British but part of something bigger. America was already voting in hard-line politicians like George W Bush but Obama was waiting in the wings with a more positive outlook in mind. In Germany, Angela Merkel was working to create a multicultural society. The world was really moving in a direction I liked and I felt happy about life.

But when we reached the year 2000, we seemed to have come to a peak – we had reached the top of that evolution pyramid; the only way to go from there was down.

Many through history have said the year 2000 was going to mark the end of the world – perhaps they were half right:

- Hal Lindsey, whose 1988 prediction failed, suggests the end in his recently published book, entitled Planet Earth – 2000 A.D. However, he leaves himself a face-saving outlet: "Could I be wrong? Of course. The Rapture may not occur between now and the year 2000." (Lindsey p. 306)
- The beginning of Christ's Millennium according to some Mormon literature, such as the publication Watch and Be Ready: Preparing for the Second Coming of the Lord. The New Jerusalem will descend from the heavens in 2000, landing in Independence, Missouri. (McIver #3377, Skinner p. 100)
- Nineteenth century mystic Madame Helena Petrova Blavatsky, the founder of Theosophy, foresaw the end of the world in 2000. (Shaw p. 83)
- Even Sir Isaac Newton was bitten by the millennium bug. He predicted that Christ's Millennium would begin in the year 2000 in his book

Observations upon the Prophecies of Daniel, and the Apocalypse of St. John. (Schwartz p. 96)
- Ruth Montgomery predicts Earth's axis will shift and the Antichrist will reveal himself in 2000. (Kyle p. 156, 195)
- The establishment of the Kingdom of Heaven, according to Rev. Sun Myung Moon. (Kyle p. 148)
- The Second Coming, followed by a New Age, according to famed psychic Edgar Cayce. (Hanna p. 219)
- The Second Coming, as forecasted in Ed Dobson's book The End: Why Jesus Could Return by A.D. 2000.
- The end of the world according to Lester Sumrall in his book I Predict 2000. (Abanes p. 99, 341)
- The tribulation is to occur before the year 2000, said Gordon Lindsay, founder of the Christ for the Nations Ministry. (Abanes p. 280)
- According to a series of lectures given by Shoko Asahara in 1992, 90% of the world's population would be annihilated by nuclear, biological and chemical weapons by the year 2000. (Thompson p. 262)

Quotes (above) courtesy of www.abhota.info

Others spoke of the millennium bug which they thought might stop computers from working, causing chaos around the world. Planes might fall from the sky when their systems failed. Of course, as we now know, the computers carried on working and life seemed to go on as usual.

But in fact, there were changes going on in secret; dark terrorist forces were plotting attacks from their hiding places in Afghanistan and Pakistan. The year 2000 saw the beginning of a massive change in our thinking because in 2001 planes really did fall from the sky!

The 9/11 terrorist attack on New York

Many say that the reason for Brexit was because we didn't like being talked down to by Brussels; maybe that's true. Some say being part of the European Union was costing us too much money; maybe that was true as well. But the hatred and racism aimed towards immigrants living in the UK since that vote tell another story.

As a way of explaining their prejudice towards foreigners, some people like to say things like: "they are taking our jobs" or "our country is full already." But I believe Islamic terrorism is the fundamental cause of the mind set many now hold around the world. Suddenly foreigners are bad – foreigners are dangerous and foreigners are unwelcome. When your very culture is threatened, when your children are at risk of being blown up at a pop concert, when your after-work drink on a Friday night suddenly turns in to a bloodbath; people start to get scared and that is why I believe after 9/11 things began to change. Suddenly there were 'others' and others were not welcome, others were bad.

The Star Trek Vision of a Multi-Racial Utopia

"… Star Trek today is an egalitarian, pluralistic, moral future society that has rejected greed and hate for the far more noble purpose of learning all that is learnable and spreading freedom throughout the galaxy. That doesn't exactly chime with the world we live in: one that is increasingly polarised, violent, and arguably teeming with existential despair. Star Trek was born out of the era of John F Kennedy, the space race, a well-educated middle class and a sense in America that anything was possible. Of course, underneath that attitude was the threat of the atomic bomb, the simmering tensions of the civil rights conflict, gender inequality and growing anger at the Vietnam War. Star Trek's creative brains trust – Roddenberry, Gene Coon, DC Fontana, John DF Black and a who's who of science fiction luminaries – was marvellously adept at grappling with these issues and, through the course of 44 minutes plus commercials, convincing the audience that intelligent, progressive minds could work together to solve any problem." Dave Schilling: The Observer

So it was on June 26th, 2016, that I sat and wept as it was announced we were leaving Europe. We were leaving togetherness, solidarity, multiculturalism and being part of a collective society.

Then Teresa May came into power (a weak prime minister who was influenced by right-wingers in her party) and we began the slide into isolationism, nationalism, intolerance, racism and hate. Now Boris Johnson and Reece Moggs are 'in charge' and I cry for my country because I believe we have lost our way; we as humans are better off together. But this way of looking at the world is not just about us Brits, it's been happening all over the world. As wars began to break out due to the rise of the Islamic State, refugees began flooding into Europe. First of all, countries like Germany tried to hold onto their principles of multiculturalism and welcomed them with open arms, but soon even Merkel had to give way, and racial intolerance now rules the day.

Then, of course, there is Trump!

If there is one figure that perfectly sums up the current world mind-set of intolerance, then it is Donald Trump; the fact that a nation like the USA can get to a point where they are prepared to elect someone like that bigot as president, says it all.

The Star Trek Vision of a Multi-Racial Utopia

Captain Kirk, Mr Spock and Dr McCoy often thought their way out of a situation, rather than simply blasting everything in sight. That's an inherently liberal position to take: but there are still conservatives among us who project their own ideas on to the series.

Barack Obama is a well-known Star Trek fan, but so is Texas senator and former presidential candidate Ted Cruz, who told the New York Times Magazine last year: "It is quite likely Kirk is a Republican." He also compared William Shatner's portrayal of Kirk to that of Star Trek: The Next Generation's Captain Jean-Luc Picard, as played by Sir Patrick Stewart. 'Kirk is working class; Picard is an aristocrat. Kirk is a passionate fighter for justice; Picard is a cerebral philosopher.' One could be forgiven for thinking he had substituted Kirk for himself and Picard for Obama. Such is the stereotype of Republicans (rugged adventurers) and Democrats (stuffy twits) in the US.

"In that same interview," Cruz said: "The original Star Trek pressed for racial equality, which was one of its best characteristics, but it did so without sermonising.' That's a peculiar way to look at the show, considering Star Trek featured the first interracial kiss on American TV and numerous episodes were allegories about the evils of racism – specifically the episode Let That Be Your Last Battlefield, an unsubtle instalment from the third and final season in which aliens with half-white and half-black faces squabble over their skin-colour differences."

But there is still hope as the 900,000+ marching in London showed. There are people who still hold onto that Star Trek ideal. There are some places that have kept their faith in mankind. The reason I love India so much is for that very reason. Despite a violent birth to their independent nation, the Indians live side by side now with all religions, cultures and outlooks. They believe very much in a collective community, all as one family.

In his book Kaleidoscope City, Piers Moore Ede writes about the Indian city of Varanasi:

"Perhaps for all of us there is a country, and within that a single place, in which some essential element of the world is illuminated for the first time. Sitting down on a park bench in a beam of sunlight, or lost in the cacophony of a spice market, it comes to us that we have never been this vibrantly, persuasively alive... the simplicity of life in the old medieval alleys, the poetry of the city's rituals and beliefs, seemed to me to represent the best of India, the best, perhaps, of the human condition."

The world is a constantly changing place and I too believe in mankind and I hope, no I believe, that in the end common sense will prevail and we will grow tired of hate, intolerance and that inward-looking mentality that has engulfed much of the world today. We are all human beings, let's embrace that and boldly go forward towards a better more collaborative community/one-family outlook and a positive way of being. Let's help that Star Trek vision of a multi-racial utopia come true:

Mark A Altman, a screenwriter, producer and lifelong Star Trek fan who recently wrote The Fifty-Year Mission: The Complete Uncensored & Unauthorized Oral History of Star Trek, notes the strong connection between Star Trek's vision and the liberal ideals of JFK. 'Star Trek was born in the crucible of the '60s when society was questioning many of the tried-and-true conservative '50s values they once took for granted,' he says. The show was born in the era of the space race and John F Kennedy's 'New Frontier'.

"'It's not an accident that James T Kirk was an analogue of John Fitzgerald Kennedy, nor that the final frontier was indeed a thinly veiled extension of Kennedy's New Frontier,' he says, referring to the slogan popularised by JFK during the 1960s presidential campaign. During a time in which mankind was questioning the very fact as to whether there would be a future in the wake of the hydrogen bomb and nuclear proliferation, and the assassinations of JFK, Martin Luther King and Robert Kennedy, Star Trek definitively said not only would there be a future, but mankind would endure and flourish."

Star Trek's 50-year mission: to shine a light on the best of humankind
By Dave Schilling: The Observer

*

The Hindu Kali Yuga

"The Kali Yuga, the fourth and last age in the cycle of ages, characterised by strife and degeneration." From Journeys in the Kali Yuga by Aki Cederberg

Are We Living in the Kali Yuga?

This article is from upliftconnect.com by Jacob Devaney

Ancient Wisdom on the Cycle of Time

"It isn't hard to recognize that even though we live on a planet that surrounds us with beauty, there is a lot of darkness happening within humanity. The ancient Sanskrit teachings understood that civilization goes through distinct cycles of creation and destruction. Native traditions have similar stories to describe different ages of humanity as well. It can be easy to lose hope sometimes, but there are many possibilities for spiritual growth and awakening during this time.

Let's look at the bigger picture knowing that the warm glow of dawn always follows the coldest, darkest moments of the night."

What Is a Yuga?

"The ancients understood time as a circle, not linear, and the circle of ages are known as the yugas. Like the four seasons in our year, there are four yugas in the full cycle (Mahayuga). Each cycle has distinct themes and spiritual lessons for humanity. Below are the four yugas in order from beginning to end. It is important to note that the first yuga is the longest with each one getting successively shorter (4:3:2:1) until the cycle starts again."

The ancients understood time as a circle.

- Satya Yuga: First we see the time of truth and perfection, which thankfully lasts four tenths of the cycle. These humans are honest, youthful, vigorous, and virtuous. Everyone is happy, and religions live as one. Disease in non-existent, as is fear. Those living through this part of the cycle are gifted with abundance through the land, along with great weather.
- Treta Yuga: The second Yuga lasts for three tenths of the cycle. Unfortunately, this is where human virtue begins to fall away. Leaders gain more dominance, causing wars to rise. As if to reflect the state of

humanity, the weather also moves to more extremes. It is unsurprising that people's health begins to lessen in this part of the cycle."

- Dvapara Yuga: The third Yuga lasts for two tenths of the cycle. During this time, people become more sluggish and slower, many aren't as strong as their ancestors, and the number of diseases increases. Becoming discontent with their lives, humans fight each other. This could possibly be because maturity decreases, with some people still possessing characteristics of youth in old age.
- Kali Yuga: The final age lasts only one tenth of the cycle, however, that is certainly long enough as it is the age of darkness and ignorance. People slide further down the path of dishonesty, with virtue being of little value. Passions become uncontrollable as unrestrained sexual indulgences and manipulations run through society. Liars and hypocrites rise. Important knowledge is lost and scriptures become less and less common. The human diet is now 'dirty', and people are not even close to being as powerful as their ancestors in the Satya Yuga. Likewise, the once pristine environment is now polluted. Water and food become scarce, as do family bonds."

The description of the Kali Yuga above is frighteningly accurate when you think about the state of our current politics and the environmental issues we are facing. But we should remember, and history has shown us this, that nothing bad ever lasts. It takes things to get really bad before people start waking up and things finally begin to change. Look at what led to the hippie movement of the '60s: political assassinations such as JFK, the Vietnam War and the communist witch hunts that were taking place in America. The reaction to that was flower power.

What Should We Do?

"It could be that we are currently in the Kali Yuga stage of the cycle. If that is true, what can we do to move back into the first, much more pleasant phase?

"The Vedic Scriptures, of course, recommend meditation, yoga, and various spiritual practices as the natural antidote to the strife of the Kali Yuga. And while some scholars have attempted to tie dates of these cycles to the calendar, yet few agree on when the Kali Yuga will end. For this reason, we must not fall into fatalism (thinking that we are all doomed and there's nothing we can do about it) or hopelessness, but instead must strengthen our personal practice and act as a light in dark times for those around us that are lost. To find peace in peaceful times is no accomplishment, to find peace in the most unpeaceful times is true spiritual attainment!

"This is one of many stories that illustrate what each of us observe when we pay close attention to nature. Life goes in natural cycles of gestation, birth, growth, decay, death, and rebirth. We see it in the plants, the seasons, in the rise and fall of nations, as well as in our own personal lives. When something is pure, it can be maintained as pure but cannot become more pure, it can only become less pure. In that same regard, when things are polluted or corrupted, they can be returned to purity. The Kali Yuga is as good a time for spiritual discipline and evolution as any.

"Something pure can be maintained but cannot become purer, it can only become less pure."

A Universal Story

"The ancient Greeks called these four ages of human civilization the Age of Gold, Silver, Bronze, and the Age of Iron. The Phoenix always rises from the ashes of its predecessor. The Hopi tribe believe that a cycle when humans head and heart are disconnected (Fourth World of Separation) is followed by an era when they are in harmony (Fifth World of Peace). The Lakota believe that the birth of a White Buffalo in 1994 signified a time of great healing and unification around the world. The Pan-American prophecy of the Eagle and Condor speaks of the re-uniting of the tribes through sacred wisdom and power. For as much darkness as one might see in the world, there are endless stories of rebirth to explore. These are roadmaps for us from the darkness into the light."

A Parable

"Once a king asked his wise men to give him something that would make him happy when he is sad, and sad when he is happy. The wise men spent days thinking about it in silence and watching the clouds go by. On the fourth day, they wrote on a piece of paper and handed it to the king. When the king read it, he thanked them. What did it say?

'This, too, shall pass.'"

– From an article by Jacob Devaney, upliftconnect.com

The Big Picture

"Whether you take this information as literal or metaphorical, you can gain much value from considering it. Destruction is part of creation; we live in a world of endless cycles. Sometimes things have to fall apart in order to come back together stronger than before. If we are actually living in the Kali Yuga now, then any and all behaviour that is wholesome, honest, generous, virtuous, happy and authentic is emulating behaviours that bring us closer to the Satya Yuga. Satya Yuga is the next phase in the cycle – a golden age of abundance. Knowing that the Kali Yuga can end abruptly at any moment, observe what is happening around you, grow your compassion, and learn what you can from this precious time!" Quotes from Jacob Devaney – from upliftconnect.com.

So you see, there is hope for humanity and if we can learn to be more tolerant, more accepting of other cultures, more loving and recognise the importance of togetherness, things will improve. If we can only try to understand each other, learning to build on friendship and join together at gatherings such as festivals (places that are full of love and togetherness), then things will improve.

If we can recognise the importance of spirituality, music, travel and saving the planet through our own actions and working hard at saving the environment – think about what we eat and the effect that has on the planet... then we have a chance of saving our world and moving on from the Kali Yuga cycle.

"Hindus believe time is cyclical. Yeah, there are some smart, technologically advanced people around today. But it's happened before. History repeats itself. Civilizations arise, work their way towards greatness, and eventually (and inevitably!) are destroyed. History hits the 'restart' button, and the process begins again." From Hinduism for Idiots by Linda Johnsen

Karma

"Karma is the Hindu view of causality in which good deeds, words, thoughts, and commands lead to beneficial effects for a person, and bad deeds, words, thoughts, and commands lead to harmful effects. These effects are not necessarily immediate but can be visited upon a soul in future lives through reincarnation; additionally, good or bad fortune experienced in life may be the result of good or bad actions performed in a past life. One's karmic state affects the reincarnation of the soul: good karma may lead to reincarnation as a human while bad karma can lead to reincarnation as an animal or other forms of non-human life. Many Hindus hold a theistic view of karma in which a personal god – such as Vishnu in Vaishnavism and Shiva in Shaivism – is responsible for administering karma according to a soul's actions. Non-theistic strands of Hinduism believe that karma is a matter of basic cause-and-effect without the need of a deity to mediate the effects." source: berkleycenter.georgetown.edu

My own reaction to this is that it contains some strange ideas. The belief that being reincarnated as an animal is a form of spiritual punishment is a strange one. As I see it animals are beautiful creatures and to be reborn as one is far from being a punishment but an honour. Sometimes I think an Earth where humans have left this planet, taking with them their destruction, pollution and war and leaving nature and animals to inherit the world would result in a much more sustainable and long-term future for this remarkable place we call home. But that's not fair to humans, because I believe we too have the ability to evolve and change for the better. "Karma is a core concept in the Indian religions, including Buddhism, Jainism, and Sikhism, although their specific views on karma vary. In Hinduism, karma is the force of retributive justice that compels believers to behave righteously according to Dharma – the moral order of the universe. As such, karma is a central component of the Hindu ethical worldview. Further, because Hindu religious ordinances govern not just the individual believer but society as a whole, belief in karma enforces and perpetuates systems of social organization prescribed in Hindu scriptures. Karma also bolsters active worship on the part of believers, as many Hindus hold that bad karma can be counteracted through ritual activity including religious pilgrimages, temple worship, and making offerings to the gods." Article source: berkleycenter.georgetown.edu

To me the answer is simple: people power will always win through – embrace the idea of Karma and embrace a new mind-set. This is the hippie Kushi outlook.

I have not given up on this world and nor should you.

*

Chapter Eight
Being Hippie Kushi

Hopefully, by now you can recognise that by getting yourself out there, overcoming your comfort zone concerns and experiencing these wonderful and life-changing clubs and festivals, you have already broadened your horizons.

On my first visits to Whirl-y-Gig I met Geoff, James, Melissa, Las and Louise and we are now all good friends. By getting myself out there instead of sitting at home watching TV, I suddenly found I have a whole new set of friends; it's easier than you think. You then start meeting these new friends at bars, clubs, house parties and festivals and before you realise it your social life is becoming exciting and fun. You may find you start to dress in a new way too and eventually you will build your own hippie style.

My new friend Louise often says to me, 'Do you fancy this trance club or this bar?'

I would think, 'Um, not sure if I will like that?'

But I will still go anyway and end up loving it. By stepping out of that comfort zone barrier you will meet more and more new people as well as regularly meeting up with the friends you made previously.

As I soon found, getting yourself out there also means you are listening to some new and exciting music, such as psytrance, Drum n Bass and World music and you start to feel elated and alive; you have woken up!!!

Having regular interactions with other hippie types will also almost certainly start you off thinking about other elements of your life, such as your diet; how does what you eat affect you and the planet. You will become more environmentally aware and spiritual, your artistic side will start to blossom.

Instead of complaining about politicians, the environment, Brexit and Trump from your sofa, you will suddenly find yourself pounding the streets of London on a protest march with your new friends and you will find yourself feeling strong, fulfilled and powerful.

We are only halfway through this book but I bet you are already feeling Hippie Kushi.

What Does It Mean to Live a Hippie Kushi Life?

Some might say I'm a little bit mad, some would say eccentric; I think I'm a product of my own difficult childhood as well as my early experiences in London. I have also been changed by my travels around the world and the influence of the people I have fondly called my friends. We are all unique but some of us just happen to live in a parallel universe where it's hard to live a 'normal' life; our minds are constantly on fire.

"Poet-metropolitan subjects reject the homeland to shape an alternative lifestyle. They become artists, therapists, exotic traders and bohemian workers seeking to integrate labour, mobility and spirituality within a cosmopolitan culture of expressive individualism." Global Nomads – Anthony D'Andrea.

Let's go back to January 2019 – it was a new year and it was looking like it was going to be a turbulent one for the UK. But for me, this was looking to be an important year. 2019 was the year I really truly embraced my new Hippie Kushi life and started achieving my goals.

As I have previously explained I had been held back from achieving my goals over the past few years by my debt issues but by the end of 2019, I would have finally conquered that particular demon. Thanks to a debt relief order my debts would be written off; freeing me from that particular ball and chain. I now wanted to move forward in my search for happiness. A new phase in my life was beginning; it was time to embrace my Hippie Kushi life.

First of all, I planned to build on my own business projects; namely my online and market stall hippie clothing and jewellery company. Also the publishing and earnings from my books along with selling my art work would build up new income sources on top of my new job at the health centre. Working a full-time job and running my own projects would be on a temporary basis as I believe it's not sustainable long term. A couple of years should do it. My flat in Hampton near Surrey is lovely but expensive to run, not allowing me to save up for the future, so extra income will help.

For some, setting up their own business might be a bit scary, but something like this doesn't faze me at all; in fact it's an exciting adventure. The only problem is I have never learnt to drive and a van would be a necessity for the business. I have now received my provisional licence and will be starting driving lessons soon; now that is scary.

About that boat, yes, eventually I would love to move on to a canal boat – it has been my dream for decades. The thought of living a laid-back life on this country's picturesque canal network fills me with peace and warmth. The canal boat community in the UK is a unique and heart-warming thing – full of people who actually communicate with each other, share their lives, show generosity, kindness and a sense of belonging. I want to be around like-minded people such as this instead of putting up with my own company day in day out and live a life with purpose.

As well as my long-term goal of living on that canal boat, my other big dream is to travel the world with just a backpack on my back and no real plans as to where I will go. I want to travel for about six months to a year. That would mean sub-letting my flat. Once I have completed those travels and I have comfortably moved onto my canal boat, I would like to spend the summers here running my market business and writing more books and in the winter spend four or five months every year in Goa; this would really make me smile.

First things first though; my short-term goal is simply to begin achieving my dreams with a real sense of direction and forward momentum – a commitment to finding contentment living a Hippie Kushi life.

But what does living a Hippie Kushi life mean? I associate myself with the word hippie because I love the hippie mind-set, the outlook and the ideal of love, freedom and togetherness. God knows we need it in a world of Donald Trump and Brexit.

I also love all the music associated with that hippie vibe – I like the clothes, the idea of living in communities and the drive to travel and embrace new cultures and religions.

But I do not believe in 'shoulds' and 'musts' – I am not a vegan or even a vegetarian although my meat intake is the lowest it's ever been. Vegans who force their politics on others are simply damaging their own cause; I believe we will naturally move in that direction as time goes by anyway.

So, let's now explore some of the aspects of Hippie Kushi life and ask the question; what is happiness and how can we achieve an alternative lifestyle that not only works but also makes us happy?

"Hippie Is a State of Mind"

The blogger known as Rich wrote about this subject in his popular blog 'living at latitude 38 and 61':

"An old mountain rescue buddy of mine, Steve Patchett, once said, 'Hippie is a state of mind.' Now I don't think he originated that phrase, but he definitely set the example – maybe not all the time, but being hippie is something to strive for, like Nirvana.

My take-away from what Steve said is that you don't have to have long hair and smoke dope to be a hippie. It's the choices about how you live your life and how your mind views your world that gives one a hippie perspective.

I do not claim to be the spokesperson for hippies (I can only speak for the hippie in me) and don't claim that I know everything about being hippie, but I have walked the hippie path for parts of my life and it is a mind-set that I embrace. The whole free love thing aside (I think all would agree that all things, especially love, have consequences), what does it mean to be hippie in this day and age? What can we do to be more hippie? How can we get ourselves back to the garden, so to speak?" **From the blog 'living at latitude 38 and 61'**

Diet:

I do believe that going vegetarian is the best way to go. Animals deserve to live out their lives without being killed and then eaten by us and meat farming harms the environment in many ways. A good example is the burning of the rain forests in Brazil to clear the way for soy crops. That soy is being grown to create feed for cattle that eventually end up as beef in products like Burger King's burgers. I only eat fish and chicken now but I eat less and less every day simply because my conscience says 'no'. It's also been suggested that eating processed meats like bacon, sausages and ham are a probable cause of cancer, so cutting these out is defiantly advisable.

I think it also helps if you are a reasonable cook (like me with my background in catering), so that you can rustle up some pretty good and tasty vegetarian food.

On top of this, growing your own fruit and vegetables is a good way to go. Eating something you have grown yourself is very satisfying. Of course, you need to have a garden or allotment to do this which not all of us have. I do not have either a garden or an allotment – I personally have never had green fingers and any attempts in the past at growing flowers on my balcony have ended in disaster. But I like the idea of growing your own fruit and vegetables; it will save the planet and cut down on plastic container use, provide food for the table and save money in doing so and I think this would help us all move towards a more healthy diet.

I think that within the next couple of years I will be completely vegetarian and there is something quite comforting in growing your own.

Opening Your Mind and Opening Your Horizons:

Turn off that TV! That box in the corner of your room is a cancer that feeds you false or bias information. The dribble of reality TV is no alternative to getting out and socialising for real, or reading a good book or listening to some great music. Try picking up a paintbrush or a pencil and creating some art, cook something special or visit an elderly neighbour for a chat; even sitting and meditating can leave you feeling exhilarated and open to new possibilities. Do things that will open up your mind; TV? You don't need it.

That said, there are sometimes programmes that are worth a watch, those rare programs with a soul and a conscience, programmes around subjects that can't be missed. Set the record for these special programs – there's not many of them but they are worth a watch. But all other times steer clear; it will change your life.

Enjoy Nature and the Beautiful Countryside:

The countryside, wherever you may live, is truly beautiful; the hills and mountains, the forests and lakes, the rivers and the wildlife. God knows I have come to appreciate it since I woke up to life. In the UK there is countryside aplenty and its truly breath-taking (have you been to the Highlands; wow!).

If you want to hug a tree, hug a tree – if you want to lie on your back in a sunny meadow and look at the beauty of the clouds, do it. If you want to sit by a river smoking a joint whilst listening to music, light it up. Get in your campervan, or your boat, or on a train and get out there and embrace the natural beauty of our countryside – take a deep breath in and smile; you will feel truly alive.

Create Your Own Power:

Alternative energy sources, now, I am not in a position to do this in my housing association flat at present but once I am in my canal boat I most definitely will be. With these alternative ways of making power, your energy costs will plummet and you are once again helping the environment. Wind turbines create plenty of power and if you live on a boat, hydropower is an option (if on a smaller scale than industrial turbines). Solar panels work very well, even in winter and are easy to install and are a huge money saver and if they also help lower emissions and save the planet; surely it's a win-win situation.

Be Spiritual:

I have found a lot of solace from studying different religions, especially Buddhism and Hinduism. It really opens your mind to consider the possibilities of these teachings. Spirituality and religion are not necessarily the same thing. I class myself as spiritual and have my own beliefs about god. Spirituality, especially in the Hindu faith, is about togetherness, all things equal and good karma (your deeds in this life will have an influence on who or what you are in the next life). Meditation is a form of spirituality and helps me greatly in my day-to-day life.

Travel the World:

Travel is one of the greatest mind expanders and a great way to move from one chapter in your life to the next. To experience different cultures and landscapes is truly inspiring. If you are a people person like me, backpacking around the world will not only let you grow as a person but gives you the opportunity to meet like-minded souls from all over the planet. A great example of this is the Ampora night market in Goa. I sat at a long table there eating delicious samosas with people from every corner of the globe; it was fantastic; you haven't lived if you haven't travelled.

Don't Get Hung Up on Race or Sexual Orientation:

One thing I love about Whirl-y-Gig is that no one bats an eyelid when two men embrace and kiss. And they shouldn't – it doesn't matter – they are not harming you and just want to live their lives to the full as much as you do. Many of us have been brought up that gay people are not 'normal' (I was and I'm gay) but we are not our parents or our peers – we are free souls that are adult enough to have an open mind and spirit. It's the same with race – what the hell difference it makes what colour skin someone has; we are all human brothers and sisters in the big cooking pot of life. Ease up, open up and love your fellow man (and woman).

Love:

On the subject of love, my crowd from whirly is full to the brim with this love stuff; I feel loved every day. In fact all of the friends I have, from my university mates to my lifelong friends, all offer unconditional love to me and me to them. If you just love everyone it's the perfect starting point to connect with others. Some might give you cause to change that opinion later but at least you gave it a go. To hate someone because of the colour of their skin, race, religion or sexuality makes no sense; it's just others influencing your judgement. Try loving them instead and see how good that feels; that love will turn into tolerance and acceptance and eventually togetherness; it's the Hippie Kushi way.

"Hippie Is a State of Mind"

Living at Latitude 38 and 61 says: "Okay, so about that smoking dope thing. Hippies were rejecting the values of their parents' generation. They even rejected their parents' drug of choice. Alcohol is abused just as much as weed. Weed, on the other hand, is something that individuals could grow for personal consumption so as not to support 'the man' who makes money in the beer and liquor industry nor would it support the illegal drug trade. I don't imbibe, but I would support legalization and taxation of weed. I also think that when people get their AARP card in the mail, it should come with a medical marijuana card to take the edge off of getting older. So there you have it: Peace, Love, Dope and a whole lot more. Walk the hippie path. Embrace the mind-set. As for me, I have built my own house. I grow a garden. I make my own energy and cut my own firewood. I embrace science and peace. I'm wary of the man. I vote, pay taxes and don't try to shirk jury assignment. I love my black, white, brown, yellow, red, gay, lesbian, transgender and straight friends and family. I've been without cable TV since 2006 but I do love me some Netflix. I share, I give thanks and most of all, I love. Thanks for the advice, Steve." Source: Living at latitude 38 and 61

These concepts are all positive aspirations and we could all be a little more 'hippie'.

"Finding [the hippie] 'It' also required one to disassociate themselves completely from white middle-class hegemonic culture and its attendant acquisitive values, oppressive ethics, and rational analysis; its grand expectations, and phoney aspirations. It could only be found by living in the impulsive moment of immediacy; by engaging in ethereal flights of 'fancy, sensuality, and community'. Perhaps most important to both Beats and Hippies, their respective collective. It could only be discovered by a devotion to authentic experience at all times in one's life." The Hippies a 1960s History – John Anthony Morella.

Happiness:

Eight Ways to Ignite Your Inner Happiness
By Claire Charters
Your life is your message to the world; make it inspiring by becoming the happiest person you know. But, how?

1. Look for Opportunities – things will not just fall in your lap; you have to go out, work hard, and earn them. In the process, you will make mistakes, however, instead of giving up, find a way that works. When you search long enough, opportunities will come your way. Be bold, tell the universe what you want. Yes, you may get a hundred 'no's' but you will eventually get one 'yes'. You will be surprised how often the universe says 'yes'! You just have to ask first.

2. Set Your Intention – manifestation is extremely powerful, so get focused on setting your intent. By getting clear about what you want and sending out positive thoughts/feelings/emotions about it, you will find the key to fulfilling your dreams. Write your own personal mantra; then hang it where you will see it every day.
3. Dream Big, and Take Risks – it is your birth right to live how you choose; dare to live it. Yes, it takes courage, because way to often you get belittled by small-minded people telling you, 'you're just a dreamer' or 'that's an impossible dream'. The people who achieve their goals are the ones who never give up, even when it seems all so hopeless.
4. Love, Nurture and Honour Yourself – speak to yourself with kindness, nourish your body with whole foods, and honour your value by living life by your own morals. Take some time to invest in the most important thing – YOU.

The True and the False Self:

"One of the most surprising but powerful explanations for why we may, as adults, be in trouble mentally is that we were, in our earliest years, denied the opportunity to be fully ourselves, that is, we were not allowed to be wilful and difficult, we could not be as demanding, aggressive, intolerant, and unrestrictedly selfish as we needed to be. Because our caregivers were preoccupied or fragile, we had to be preternaturally attuned to their demands, sensing that we had to comply in order to be loved and tolerated; we had to be false before we had the chance to feel properly alive. And as a result, many years later, without quite understanding the process, we risk feeling unanchored, inwardly dead and somehow not entirely present."

Source: www.theschooloflife.com

What the writer is talking about here are our true and false selves. So many of us go about life being somebody we are not, unconsciously or otherwise putting on an act; if we could only learn to be our real, true selves, we would find pure happiness.

"This psychological theory of the True and the False Self is the work of one of the twentieth century's greatest thinkers, the English psychoanalyst and child psychiatrist Donald Winnicott. In a series of papers written in the 1960s and based on close observations of his adult and infant patients, Winnicott advanced the view that healthy development invariably requires us to experience the immense, life-sustaining luxury of a period when we do not have to bother with the feelings and opinions of those who are tasked with looking after us. We can be wholly and, without guilt, our True Selves, because those around us have – for a time – adapted themselves entirely to our needs and desires, however inconvenient and arduous these might be." Source: www.theschooloflife.com

But what if, as well as having a 'true self' period in young childhood we could also return to our true selves in later life. Once again being free to be naughty, playful and have a good time. Living life whilst projecting a false self only breeds unhappiness and many of us live that way without even realising it. Be true to yourself; don't be afraid to be who you want to be. If you want to dye your hair a bright pink or grow it long, wear colourful clothes or have tattoos and piercings; do it! Never worry about being who you really are. Others may voice their opinions but unless 'you' are true to yourself you may never find happiness.

Kindness:

"Generosity boosts reward mechanisms in the brain. Everybody can appreciate acts of kindness. But when it comes to explaining why we do them, people often take one of two extreme positions. Some think kindness is something completely selfless that we do out of love and care, while others believe it is just a tool that we cunningly use to become more popular and reap the benefits. But research shows that being kind to others can actually make us genuinely happy in a number of different ways. We know that deciding to be generous or others activates an area of the brain called the striatum. Interestingly, this area responds to things we find rewarding, such as nice food and even addictive drugs. The feel-good emotion from helping has been termed 'warm glow' and the activity we see in the striatum is the likely biological basis of that feeling. Of course, you don't have to scan brains to see that kindness has this kind of benefit. Research in psychology shows a link between kindness and well-being throughout life, starting at a very young age. In fact, even just reflecting on having been kind in the past may be enough to improve teenagers' mood. Research has also shown that spending extra money on other people may be more powerful in increasing happiness than spending it on yourself. But why and how does kindness make us so happy? There are a number of different mechanisms involved, and how powerful they are in making us feel good may depend on our personalities." Source: theconversation.com

"Helping someone makes you smile and smiling makes you feel happy."

Multiculturalism and Togetherness:

"We all need each other to live in positive energy. This is a world subtly divided in negativity where doubts rule and fear conquers the anxious minds. At such times, only our unity will help us. Unity of whom? Unity of those who have the strength to live without fear in such times. There are individuals and groups who have conquered the limitations of adversity and dominance of negativity and set a prime example of what it is to live. Who haven't lost hope and fought each moment to give everyone an example to cherish for. It is indeed these people who make life look worth living. It is in remembrance and understanding of these minds, their thoughts that can act as catalyst and bring about a change that can last for long. The world needs a peaceful model – a successful model. A model that can guide how to live beyond conflicts and prosper. In the absence of this all can be said is, 'United we can prosper, divided we wander…' let's come together and build together a peaceful society, a United society!" Source: medium.com

Inner Peace, Having Fun, Partying and Attending Festivals

It may seem strange to lump these things together but they all have the same result if done correctly.

Meditation and yoga are great things to practice. I meditate every day and it has a wonderful effect on my stress disorder. You shouldn't dismiss it unless you've tried it. It can calm you down, counteract nerves, free your mind and refresh you.

Partying and socialising can do wonders for your soul. You are never too old to party and my life was changed forever after dancing on the beaches of Goa with other 'older' hippies.

But don't go about it the wrong way; too much drug-taking or drinking every night will have a counteractive effect and bring you down: know your limits.

Festivals are the single best way to meet like-minded people. The atmosphere is like a parallel universe to the outside world; plenty of togetherness, harmony, love and joy.

Conclusion in a Quote:

"What I've learnt is that no one will encourage you to have a different or interesting life. Doing a dream is what makes life interesting and exciting, but it can be a lonely pursuit in the beginning. And that's another reason I share what I do. So if you relate to how I felt a few years ago, know that you're not alone."
How to live in a Van – Mike Hudson vandogtraveller.com

*

Chapter Nine
Sex, Drugs and Rock and Roll

Drugs:

I wanted to start this chapter with a short look at drugs. I should say that I am by no means promoting drugs and I'm aware they are illegal and can be very damaging to peoples' lives. I certainly do not condone the taking of drugs like heroin, crack or even cocaine, as I have seen what they can do to people. But that said, drugs have come back into my life and I would like to talk about that now.

Years ago when the rave scene was at its height in the late '90s, I found myself taking a lot of drugs. First of all, I was given speed at a party we were having at the house share where I was living at the time and that quickly became something I constantly craved. Then I was taking ecstasy at night clubs which went from the odd Saturday night to several times a week. I was addicted to the high and the feeling of love it gave me and I needed more and more. Then I got into harder drugs like cocaine and quickly things got out of control and I started getting messy.

I got to the stage where things like clubbing were just not enjoyable anymore because of my addiction to party drugs. I decided to take myself away from the scene and the dealer contacts I had in London and moved in with my brother in Brighton for three years. I stopped drugs immediately and never looked back; eventually returning to London a changed man.

When I was diagnosed HIV+ in 2006 I got really down and a friend suggested marijuana. I found this really helped to relax me and without a doubt, it saved my life as I was quite suicidal at the time. When I had got used to my diagnosis and my health had improved, I moved on with my life and started working full time again. I decided eventually to stop smoking weed as I felt it had served its purpose and so I quit, just like that.

For over ten years I had not touched drugs of any form.

Then I went to Goa in India and had my life-changing experience of dancing with hippies all night on the beach. My reawakening had begun. I did not take any party drugs in India but did smoke a little weed and found the odd joint did not hurt and I have continued with that philosophy to this day.

It was when I started to go to hippie and trance clubs in the UK (I now attend many, many clubs and I am not talking about any particular venue) that I realised I had not factored in the fact that people would be taking drugs. The places I was frequenting were all-night parties and people were taking E (ecstasy) and acid just like they did in the old days so that they could party all night. But I got the impression through conversations with fellow party-goers that the pills they were now taking were a lot purer than they used to be in the '90s. Perhaps it is because the clubs I now go to have an older crowd who will only take drugs that are purer and safer.

Regardless, I was left in no doubt that drugs were a big part of this new club scene that I was embracing and I had to have a think about how I felt about that because of my past difficult experiences.

I decided after I attended my second all-night club that I would take half an E and see how I felt about it. I felt magnificent and danced all night. I was worried about the come down the next day but have never had one since I started taking E again. The difference is I only take something once a month now. I do not feel I want more than that and I am not addicted – I am a grown-up and find I do things more responsibly. I take purer, safer drugs (as safe as they can be), I don't take too much and I'm careful. This is my choice, my body and it is part of my new Hippie Kushi life. You, of course, must make up your own mind.

Sex:

During my boring grey, full stop years, I went from being a crazy sexual rabbit to not having any sex at all. I had fallen out of love with myself and saw myself as a fat, ugly, sick and an old has-been. I stopped going out on the scene and stopped even looking for possible partners. I had always been a romantic at heart, despite my promiscuity and I had always been someone who craved love and affection; but not anymore. I was happy to sit at home on my own with a bottle of wine, watching TV; what the fuck was that all about?

When I 'woke up' in India and found myself again, I also started to accept the person I was. That I was beautiful despite what my dark voices had previously been telling me. Once I had embraced my hippie self and came out of the chrysalis like a shiny Hippie Kushi butterfly, I also realised I had fallen back in love with who I am. I started attending clubs like Psymera, Whirl-y-Gig and Tribal Village and began meeting new people and before I knew it, I was snogging handsome gentlemen on the dance floor. Soon that would lead to the odd visit to my flat with someone nice for some jiggy-jiggy. After having sex again my libido returned (it had all been in my head anyway). Sex has now returned to my life.

A romantic partner, on the other hand, is something that may or may not happen one day; as I go along on this exciting journey of mine.

Let's wait and see.

Friendship:

Since embracing my new life one thing has stood out over all other aspects of my journey and that has been the friends I have made along the way (and not only that but the 'quality' of the friends I have made).

Through travel, I have always felt I have met some amazing people, probably because the sort of people that go on the sort of world adventures I go on have a certain mind-set – a certain way of being that attracts me and that I can relate to.

Whirl-y-Gig is full of people that are like that; amazing colourful souls who travel to the beaches of Goa every year, who backpack across Asia, who go to festivals and often live alternative lifestyles. They live on canal boats or in motorhomes or in community housing co-ops or shared hippie homes. They spend half the year in India or travelling around the world; people that know what life is all about and know how to really 'live'.

Through Whirl-y-Gig I have made friends now that text, message me or phone me regularly to check if I'm OK and asking how has my week been? Do I want to come over to dinner or go to the pub or even on holiday with them? It's wonderful because I lost all that during my grey years – I stayed at home and had very few friends.

I'm not saying I do not have good friends from before but these relationships are different. I only see my old friends about once every two months for a drink and a catch up because they have busy lives. But to have friends that you can hang out with each week, go clubbing with or travel together to festivals or go out to dinner is wonderful and it's lifting me up.

A perfect example and the time when I really recognised that I was surrounded by beautiful people – was when I had my Hippie Kushi party at my flat. Loads of people turned up, to my surprise, it was a real success. Not only were my whirly friends there but also some of my old university friends, as well as a work colleague from a former job. All around me were people I really care about and people I know care about me and that is magical.

Good friends are really important and something worth treasuring.

Rock and Roll:

(Embrace your love of music; it's the theme tune to your life):

Music is indeed the soundtrack to our lives; it cheers us up, makes us sad, gives us epiphanies and makes us fall in love.

Since my transition and re-awakening into the person I am today, I have come across some magnificent music; music that inspires me, music to meditate too, music to activate my creativity and music to dance all night too, music to make you feel powerful and music that is both beautiful and inspirational.

So, in the vein of this new hippie Kushi whirly world, here is my soundtrack to a hippie Kushi life!

(All information in the section below care of Wikipedia)

Transglobal Underground:

Musical collaborators since their schooldays, Tim Whelan and Hamilton Lee were previously both founding members of British pop band Furniture and had played with the experimental psychedelic art-punk group The Transmitters. While with Furniture, both musicians had already demonstrated an interest in world music by bringing in more culturally diverse instrumentation to what was originally a fairly conventional rock band line up (Lee had played tongue drums and other percussion in addition to his standard drum kit, while Whelan had supplemented his guitar playing with extensive use of the Chinese yangqin zither). Following the break-up of Furniture, Whelan and Lee worked together as part of the Flavel Bambi Septet (an Ealing-based world music band with a shifting line-up including other Transmitters members and future TGU member Natacha Atlas).

Transglobal Underground was first formed when Whelan and Lee teamed up with a third musician, Nick Page. All three took on pseudonyms for the project, which they have determinedly maintained (albeit with variations) up until the present day. Whelan became 'Alex Kasiek', Lee 'Hamid Mantu' and Page 'Count Dubulah'. The first recording by the group was the single 'Temple Head' which was shopped around various labels before eventually being released by Nation Records in 1991. Although not a major hit, it was named 'Single of the Week' in Melody Maker a publication that frequently reviewed and promoted the group, and heavily featured at clubs such as Whirl-Y-Gig. The group was quickly signed to Deconstruction Records, for whom they recorded an album.

Albums

- *International Times, 1994,*
- *Psychic Karaoke, 1996,*
- *Rejoice, 1998*
- *Yes Boss Food Corner, 2001*
- *Impossible Broadcasting, 2004*
- *Moonshout, 2007*
- *A Gathering of Strangers, 2010*
- *The Stone Turntable, 2011*
- *Kabatronics 2013*

Compilation and remix albums

- *Interplanetary Meltdown, 1995 (remix album)*
- *Backpacking on the Graves of Our Ancestors, 1999 (greatest hits album with some new tracks and mixes)*

- *Impossible Re-Broadcasting, 2007 (remix album)*
- *Run Devils and Demons, 2009 (2 CD compilation of TGU's career)*
- *Digging the Underground Volume 1: The Nation Years, 2016 (collection of unreleased tracks)*
- *Destination Overground, 2017 (compilation of TGU with Natacha Atlas and 3 new tracks)*

My Thoughts:

Transglobal Underground, with their mix of Indian, African and Arabic rhythms to a background of house music is both exhilarating and uplifting and they have definitely been my main soundtrack to my new Hippie Kushi life.

Karsh Kale:

Karsh Kale (pronounced Kursh Kah-lay, कर्ष काळे in Marathi; born November 1st 1974) is an American musician, record producer, songwriter, film composer and DJ. He is considered one of the pioneering figures in defining the Asian Underground genre by mixing disparate genres of music such as Indian classical and folk with electronica, rock, pop and ambient music. In addition to production, remixing, and DJ work, Kale is known for his tabla-drumming and film composition.

His first full-length album was Realize in 2001. Realize, often considered as a major milestone in what Kale called 'Asian Massive', was followed with 2002's Asian Massive Tour, which also featured Midival Punditz and Cheb i Sabbah, and 2003's Liberation. Zakir Hussain also was featured in the album and in the major attraction of the album 'Milan'.

Kale's third album, 2006's Broken English, was predominantly set to English lyrics, a shift from his previous albums. His follow-up Breathing Under Water, released in 2007, was the result of a two-year collaboration with sitar instrumentalist Anoushka Shankar. In 2011, Kale released Cinema, which is influenced by Kale's experiences in composing for Bollywood. He also won GIMA Awards best fusion album for the same, beating A.R.Rahman.

Solo albums

- *Realize (2001)*
- *Redesign: Realize Remixed (2002)*
- *Liberation (2003)*
- *Broken English (2006)*
- *Breathing Under Water (with Anoushka Shankar) (2007)*
- *Cinema (2010)*
- *UP (2016)*

With Tabla Beat Science

- *Tala Matrix (2000)*
- *Live at Stern Grove Palm Pictures (2003)*
- *Talaman Soundclash, Live at the Filmore (2004)*

EPs

- *Bright Like This (1999)*
- *Classical Science Fiction from India (2000)*
- *Play (1999)*
- *Pause (1999)*
- *Back Seat Lavni (1999)*
- *Distance Remixes (2000)*
- *Beautiful Remixes EP (2007)*
- *Manifest Remixes EP (2006)*

With Dave Douglas

- *Freak In (RCA, 2003)*

My Thoughts:

What a discovery Karsh Kale has turned out to be. After exploring the Whirly-Gig music channel on YouTube, I came across this artist and was immediately blown aware. Never mind soundtrack to life, many of his tracks sound like they belong in a movie with orchestral scores overlapping Indian dance music that builds up to a drum and bass and trance climax; fantastic, truly modern world music.

Jesca Hoop:

Jessica 'Jesca' Ada Hoop (born April 21st 1975 in Santa Rosa, California) is an American singer-songwriter and guitarist, who writes and performs in diverse musical styles. She has released five studio albums of her own, as well as live, acoustic and dual albums with others.

Albums by Hoop

- *Kismet (2007)*
- *Hunting My Dress (2009)*
- *The House That Jack Built (2012)*
- *The Complete Kismet Acoustic (2013) – live acoustic versions of songs mostly from Kismet*
- *Undress (2014) – acoustic reinterpretations of songs from Memories Are Now (2017)*
- *Stonechild (2019)*

Albums with Others
- Love Letter for Fire (with Sam Beam) (2016)

Eps
- Kismet Acoustic (2008)
- Snowglobe (2011)

Other

- Silverscreen Demos (2004)

My Thoughts:

This is another artist I came across by accident after searching for some Celtic music to add to my playlist. This lady is incredible, merging Irish folk music with Kate Bush-like choral backing vocals; creating a sound that is haunting, melancholy and deeply moving, beautiful quality music.

Thom Yorke:

Thomas Edward Yorke (born October 7th 1968) is an English musician and the singer and main songwriter of the alternative rock band Radiohead. A multi-instrumentalist, he mainly plays guitar and keys. Along with the other members of Radiohead, he was inducted into the Rock and Roll Hall of Fame in 2019.

Yorke was born in Northamptonshire. His family lived in Scotland before settling in Oxfordshire, England, where he formed Radiohead with his schoolmates. After he graduated from the University of Exeter, Radiohead signed to Parlophone; their early hit "Creep" made Yorke a celebrity, and Radiohead have gone on to achieve critical acclaim and sales of over 30 million albums. Their fourth album, Kid A (2000), saw Yorke and the band move into electronic music, often manipulating his vocals.

Yorke's solo work comprises mainly electronic music. His debut solo album, The Eraser, was released in 2006. To perform it live, in 2009 he formed a new band, Atoms for Peace, with musicians including Red Hot Chili Peppers bassist Flea and Radiohead producer Nigel Godrich; they released an album, Amok, in 2013. Yorke's second solo album, Tomorrow's Modern Boxes, was released in 2014, followed by Anima in 2019. He has collaborated with artists including PJ Harvey, Björk, Flying Lotus, and Modeselektor, and has composed for film and theatre; his first feature film soundtrack, Suspiria, was released in October 2018. With artist Stanley Donwood, Yorke creates artwork for Radiohead albums. He often incorporates "erratic" dancing into his performances.

Yorke is an activist on behalf of human rights, animal rights, environmental and anti-war causes, and his lyrics incorporate political themes. He has been critical of the music industry, particularly of major labels and streaming services such as Spotify. With Radiohead and his solo work he has pioneered alternative music release platforms such as pay-what-you-want and BitTorrent.

Following the OK Computer tour, he suffered a mental breakdown and found it impossible to write new music. In 2013, he said:

> "When I was a kid, I always assumed that (fame) was going to answer something – fill a gap. And it does the absolute opposite. It happens with everybody. I was so driven for so long, like a fucking animal, and then I woke up one day and someone had given me a little gold plate for OK Computer and I couldn't deal with it for ages."

To recuperate, Yorke moved to Cornwall and spent time walking the cliffs, writing and drawing. He restricted his song writing to piano; the first song he wrote was 'Everything in Its Right Place'. During this period, Yorke listened almost exclusively to the electronic music of artists such as Aphex Twin and Autechre, saying: "It was refreshing because the music was all structures and had no human voices in it. But I felt just as emotional about it as I'd ever felt about guitar music." Radiohead took these influences to their next albums Kid A (2000) and Amnesiac (2001), processing vocals, obscuring lyrics, and using electronic instruments such as synthesisers, drum machines, and samplers. The albums divided fans and critics, but were commercially successful and later attracted wide acclaim; at the turn of the decade, Kid A was named the best album of the 2000s by Rolling Stone and Pitchfork.

In 2003, Radiohead released their sixth album, Hail to the Thief, a blend of rock and electronic music. Yorke wrote many of its lyrics in response to the War on Terror and the resurgence of right-wing politics in the west after the turn of the millennium, and his shifting worldview after becoming a father. In 2007, Radiohead independently released their seventh album, In Rainbows, as a pay-what-you-want download, the first for a major act; the release made headlines worldwide and sparked debate about the implications for the music industry. In 2011, Radiohead self-released their eighth album, The King of Limbs, which Yorke described as 'an expression of physical movements and wildness'. The music video for the track 'Lotus Flower', featuring Yorke's erratic dancing, became an internet meme. Radiohead released their ninth album, A Moon Shaped Pool, on May 8th 2016. Radiohead have sold over 30 million albums.

Solo Discography:

Studio Albums:

The Eraser (2006)
Tomorrow's Modern Boxes (2014)
Anima (2019)

Film Soundtracks:

The Twilight Saga: New Moon (2009; Original Motion Picture Soundtrack; 'Hearing Damage')
When the Dragon Swallowed the Sun (2010; additional music only)
The UK Gold (2013; with Robert Del Naja)
Why Can't We Get Along (2018; Rag & Bone short film)
Time of Day (2018; Rag & Bone short film)
Suspiria (2018)

My Thoughts:

I have always quite liked Radiohead but not enough to buy their records, but Thom Yorke's solo stuff is something else. Some of his stuff is quite minimalist, just piano and/or acoustic guitar and it reminds me of the sort of acoustic hippie folk music coming out of America in the 1960s.

Then there is his other side, the stuff with a dance beat to it. His spiritual chilled out dance music; it's atmospheric, experimental and feels quite psychedelic and trippy; I love it, it's right up my street.

Ozric Tentacles:

Ozric Tentacles (also known as The Ozrics) are an English instrumental rock band, whose music incorporates elements from a diverse range of genres, including psychedelic rock, progressive rock, space rock, jazz fusion, electronic music, dub music, world music, and ambient music. Formed in Somerset in 1983, the band has released over 30 albums selling over a million copies worldwide despite never having signed to a major recording label. Throughout many line-up changes over the years, co-founder and guitarist Ed Wynne has remained the only original member of the band. The band is now credited as one of the major influences of the UK festival scene's re-emergence, becoming particularly associated with the Glastonbury Festival and their handmade series of cassette releases, mostly sold at gigs and through a fan club.

Studio albums

- *Pungent Effulgent (1989)*
- *Erpland (1990)*
- *Strangeitude (1991)*
- *Jurassic Shift (1993)*
- *Arborescence (1994)*
- *Become the Other (1995)*
- *Curious Corn (1997)*
- *Waterfall Cities (1999)*
- *The Hidden Step (2000)*
- *Swirly Termination (2000)*
- *Spirals in Hyperspace (2004)*
- *The Floor's Too Far Away (2006)*
- *The Yumyum Tree (2009)*
- *Paper Monkeys (2011)*
- *Technicians of the Sacred (2015)*

My Thoughts:

I've always quite liked the prog-rock psychedelic stuff that my brother used to play to me when I was growing up. But since going to Whirl-y-Gig I have been introduced to some exciting modern trippy rock bands like the Re-stoned and Ozric Tentacles.

The Re-stoned (also known as the Stoned) and other groups such as Dope Lemon have a much more 'stoned out' trippy feel to their music (which I love if that's the mood I'm in). This is very much the music you here on stage at the Saturday night market in Goa.

Ozric Tentacles, on the other hand, go for a much more upbeat, full-on acid trip rock sound with reggae and dance overtones. They are uplifting, exciting and perfectly fit into any party/club playlist.

OTT:

(From their Facebook page)

OTT was doomed to be a teenager in the cultural wasteland that was the mid-1980s provincial England. After a brief period wandering aimlessly through the hair sprayed deserts of New Romanticism and poodle-rock he found refuge in the warm, inviting sounds of Scientist, King Tubby, LKJ, and Prince Far-I and the effortless grace of European experimentalists Neu! and Kraftwerk. Here he stayed until he felt it was safe to pop his head up again. The end of the 1980s brought with it a cultural and musical revolution and OTT headed to London to immerse himself in the new energy. Initially unimpressed by the frantic, unmusical clatterings of acid house and "rave" he discovered a new wave of artists who apparently shared his love of organic dub and pristine electronics. Artists such as The Orb, Dub Syndicate, FSOL and African Head Charge. These were people who were unafraid to combine bass-heavy rhythm, abstract soundscape and timeless melody into a huge, ever-shifting sonic universe which reflected perfectly the spirit of hope and positivity which prevailed. It was at this point that OTT found his first work as an engineer in several studios around North London. Working obsessively, 18 hours a day, seven days a week for the next ten years, OTT began developing the skills which would see him go on to work with many of those who created the sounds which inspired him in the first place – Brian Eno, The Orb, Youth, African Head Charge, Steve Hillage, and On-U-Sound. After spending the 1990s freelancing around London as a studio engineer and producer, OTT celebrated the end of the twentieth century and the beginning of the 21st by giving it all up and moving to a remote cottage in South West England to be alone with his cats and his studio. With a vague plan to create the perfect soundtrack to an outdoor English festival he embarked on a series of sonic experiments, drawing heavily on the classic dub sounds from Jamaica and hypnotic electronic pulse from Germany which had provided such a refuge during the 1980s. A period of intense creativity followed, during which a great many tracks were created and then stashed away on tapes, seemingly never to see the light of day. In the meantime, OTT hatched a plan to remix half a dozen or so classic Hallucinogen trance tracks and release them as dub mixes – slower, fatter and more chillout friendly. In 2002 the album 'Hallucinogen in Dub' was released via Twisted Records to universal acclaim. Buoyed by the success of 'Hallucinogen in Dub', the following year OTT gathered together and released his earlier sonic experiments as the album 'Blumenkraft' which was also very well received and which attracted a great many listeners around the world. The next few years passed in a whirl of gigs, remixes (Shpongle, Entheogenic, Tripswitch) and collaborative projects – 'Umberloid' with friend and multi-instrumentalist Chris Barker, and 'Gargoyles' with Simon Posford (Hallucinogen, Shpongle). During this time OTT travelled the world, got married, welcomed his daughter Daisy to the world and wrote his third album 'Skylon' – which was released on Twisted Records in early 2008.

Studio Albums

- *Blumenkraft (2003)*
- *Skylon (2008)*
- *Mir (2011)*
- *Baby Robot EP (2013)*
- *Fairchildren (2015)*

My Thoughts:

This band is another example of the trippy spaced-out sound, perfect for the end of a party when most of the dancers have gone home. You sit with your friends on the floor, relax (with a smoke) and chill out to the psychedelic sounds of OTT.

Psytrance:

Psychedelic Trance:

Psychedelic trance, psytrance or psy is a subgenre of trance music characterised by arrangements of rhythms and layered melodies created by high tempo riffs.

Psytrance lies at the hardcore, underground end of the diverse trance spectrum. The genre offers variety in terms of mood, tempo, and style. Some examples include full on, darkpsy, forest, minimal (Zenonesque), Hitech psy, progressive, suomi, psy-chill, psycore, psybient (fusion of psychedelic trance and ambient), psybreaks, or 'adapted' tracks from other music genres. Goa trance preceded psytrance; when digital media became more commonly used psytrance evolved. Goa continues to develop alongside the other genres.

Origins:

The first hippies who arrived in Goa, India in the mid-1960s were drawn there for many reasons, including the beaches, the low cost of living, the friendly locals, the Indian religious and spiritual practices and the readily available Indian cannabis, which until the mid-1970s was legal. During the 1970s the first Goa DJs were generally playing psychedelic rock bands such as the Grateful Dead, Pink Floyd and The Doors. In 1979 the beginnings of electronic dance music could occasionally be heard in Goa in the form of tracks by artists such as Kraftwerk but it was not until 1983 that DJs Laurent and Fred Disko, closely followed by Goa Gil, began switching the Goa style over to electro-industrial/EBM which was now flooding out of Europe from Frontline Assembly, Front 242, Nitzer Ebb as well as Eurobeat.

The tracks were remixed, removing the lyrics, looping the melodies and beats and generally manipulating the sounds in all manner of ways before the tracks were finally presented to the dancers as custom Goa-style mixes.

By 1990–91 Goa was no longer under the radar and had become a hot destination for partying. As the scene grew bigger, Goa-style parties spread like a diaspora all over the world from 1993. Parties like Pangaea and Megatripolis in the UK helped spawn a multitude of labels in various countries (U.K. Australia, Japan, Germany) to promote psychedelic electronic music that reflected the ethos of Goa parties, Goa music, and Goa-specific artists, producers, and DJs. Goa Trance as commercial scene began gaining global traction in 1994. The golden age of the first wave of Goa Psy Trance as a generally agreed upon genre was between 1994–97.

Development:

By 1992 the Goa trance scene had a pulse of its own, though the term 'Goa trance' didn't become the name tag of the genre until around 1994. The Goa trance sound, which by the late 1990s was being used interchangeably with the term psychedelic trance, retained its popularity at outdoor raves and festivals, but also permanent psytrance nightclubs emerged such as Natraj Temple in Munich. New artists were appearing from all over the world and it was in this year that the first Goa trance festivals began, including the Gaia Festival in France and the still-running VuuV festival in Germany.

In 1993 the first 100% Goa trance album was released, Project II Trance, featuring tracks by Man With No Name and Hallucinogen to name two. Goa trance enjoyed its commercial peak between 1996 and 1997 with media attention and some recognised names in the DJ scene joining the movement. This hype did not last long and once the attention had died down so did the music sales, resulting in the failure of record labels, promotion networks and also some artists. This 'commercial death of Goa trance' was marked musically by Matsuri Productions in 1997 with the release of the compilation Let it RIP. On the back sleeve of the album at the bottom of the notes, R.I.P: Mother Theresa, Princess Diana, William Burroughs and Goa Trance was written.

While the genre may have been incubated in the Goa trance scene it went on to proliferate globally. Its impact was felt in Western Europe, Israel, North America, Australia, Japan and South Africa. Psytrance is linked to other music genres such as big beat, electroclash, grime and two-step. The genre evolved in conjunction with a multimedia psychedelic arts scene.

My Thoughts:

What can I say about psytrance? I have had a complete turnaround over this music. When I first investigated Goa and read about what the hippies were dancing to out there, I could not believe it was this boring melodic boom, boom, boom rubbish.

Three weeks later and I was on the beach in Anjuna having the time of my life to this fantastic, uplifting music. When you really listen to this music it is far from being just boom, boom, boom. The trance beats are overlaid with spiritual Indian sounds laced with Asian music samples and Buddhist and Hindu chanting. It's almost a religious experience; especially when you are dancing with thousands of other happy revellers.

I have been to a few places in London now that specialise in psytrance, such as Psymera and of course Whirl-y-Gig which plays a lot of psytrance mixed in with groups like Transglobal Underground and I absolutely love it now; it feels me with happiness, elation and a feeling of togetherness.

Drum n Bass:

Drum n Bass (Jungle) is a new one on me, I had realised I really enjoyed dancing to a certain beat at Whirl-y-Gig but had not associated it with D n B. It was only on the first night of the Whirl-y Fayre at the welcome party that my mind was really blown by an amazing DJs set. His name was JungleChris and the incredible music blew my mind. I danced all night and on my return home I quickly downloaded loads of this genre of music.

Also at the Fayre was a group called Loonaloop, an Australian Drum & Bass (plus many other influences) group; they were incredible. This is now my favourite kind of dance music.

Drum and bass commonly abbreviated as 'D&B', 'DnB' or 'D'n'B') is a genre and branch of electronic music characterised by fast breakbeats (typically 160–180 beats per minute) with heavy bass and sub-bass lines, sampled sources, and synthesisers.

It emerged from rave and jungle scenes in the United Kingdom during the early 1990s. The popularity of drum and bass at its commercial peak ran parallel to several other homegrown dance styles in the UK.

Drum and bass incorporates a number of scenes and styles. A major influence on jungle and drum and bass was the original Jamaican dub and reggae sound. Another feature of the style is the complex syncopation of the drum tracks' breakbeat.

Drum and bass subgenres include breakcore, ragga jungle, hardstep, darkstep, techstep, neurofunk, ambient drum and bass, liquid funk (aka liquid drum and bass), jump up, drum funk, funk step, sambas, and drill 'n' bass. From its roots in the UK, the style has established itself around the world. Drum and bass has influenced many other genres like hip hop, big beat, dubstep, house, trip hop, ambient music, techno, jazz, rock and pop. Drum and bass is dominated by a relatively small group of record labels. Major international music labels had shown very little interest in the drum and bass scene until BMG Rights Management acquired RAM in February 2016 Drum and bass remains most popular in the UK, although it has developed scenes all around the world in countries such as the United States, Germany, the Netherlands, South Africa, Belgium, New Zealand, Greece, Canada, Austria, the Czech Republic, Slovakia, and Australia.

Music is love, music is joy, music is friendship, happiness and kingship; music is the soundtrack to your life. Music is Hippie Kushi!

*

Chapter Ten
Work-Life Balance

Work and Earning vs Your Own Projects

When I was working at the NHS, I was aware of a sense of frustration. I was working up to 70 hours a week and had no time for myself or my own artistic projects. My life was work and earning and paying rent and bills and nothing else.

I decided to retire from the NHS at 55 years old as I have had enough, both physically and mentally. I now work about 35 hours a week at a local sports and health centre and I love it. Its ten minutes up the road from me, its sociable, fun and fits into my new lifestyle. It is not a case of 'this is what I do', it is simply a job that finances what I do (my stuff). I like my new job, although I would still like to work less and make more money from my own stuff which is a balance that is hard to master; so, what about these projects of mine?

We all have something we would rather be doing, be that creating music, DJ'ing, creating art and crafts or simply travelling the globe. I would love to make more art and sell it on Facebook and at markets. I have now published this book and hope to make good money from this and future books. My blog now has enough readers for me to get paid advertising if I choose and I would really like to set up my own Hippie Kushi clothing and jewellery business, both online and at a street market stall; but it's all a risk and it needs time.

The thing is if you drop your regular job hours to build up these personal projects you are at risk of struggling financially. It's a real case of the age-old work-life balance crisis; an existential struggle of work and responsibility versus being in control of your own life and future and being your own boss.

To live an ideal Hippie Kushi existence, these personal projects, these business enterprises and these natural outpourings of our artistic creativity should be the things that we eventually think of as our 'job'. We can then let go of our old life, of our 'regular job' and move into the realm of a true Hippie Kushi life.

So, what is the answer to this conundrum?

I personally believe the best approach is to keep that 'regular job' income for now, so that you have the financial security you need to keep money worries and the bailiffs away. Find time for your own projects when you can (weekends and evenings) but don't neglect them.

When you are ready, pick one single project from your portfolio (for me it would be setting up my Hippie Kushi clothing and jewellery business) and concentrate on only that one thing for now; because trying to work on too many things whilst still holding down a regular job is only going to result in failure. Bit by bit you can put your efforts into setting that project up, researching the pros, cons, where you want to sell, any licences needed, and who your market is and everything you need to know to make it a success. Eventually, when the time is right, open that business up. It will probably have to be in the evening and at the weekend to start off with but that will eventually change.

Once that project is a success and you are making money from it, you can either reduce your regular job hours to part-time or give it up altogether. See, already you are doing your thing and not working for the man.

Once your new project is really going well and you are settled into it, give up that last 'normal job' and with your new project as your financial security, start building on the next thing (for me, it would be my next book or producing a new piece of artwork to sell).

Eventually, you will realise your life is your own, you are your own master and you are free.

That said, I always think it is good to keep a 'work skill' as a backup, so that if business is slow on your own projects, you can do a few shifts to top yourself up financially (there is nothing wrong with this as you are doing it to support your own stuff). For me it would be bar work; there is always bar work to be had anywhere in the UK and most places around the world as well; it's a good back up skill to have, especially if you are a global nomad.

If you follow these ideas through, your work-life balance will now be pretty good because your 'main job' involves your own artistic projects and if they are the right kind of projects and they can be done anywhere in the world, you could then consider the next thing I am going to talk about in this book.

What if you were able to completely immerse yourself into the Hippie Kushi mind-set? Find total hippie happiness? You are now building your own creative business enterprise, growing your own artistic projects. You have freed yourself up in the way you now dress, the places you socialise and the friends you keep.

Perhaps then you could consider going the whole hog and adopting a new, exciting and different way of living; an alternative lifestyle. Perhaps you could consider living as part of a community coop or living on a canal boat or travelling the country (or world) in a campervan home. The options are endless and could change your life forever. In the next chapter, we will explore the possibilities.

*

Chapter Eleven
Live an Alternative Lifestyle

Ever say to yourself: I need a new life. Here are some alternative lifestyles and communities you might want to consider:

When I realised I needed to move on from my 'full stop' life, I started looking at the alternatives. Alternatives to working long hours, day after day at a job I was no longer enjoying. How can you escape that aimless treadmill? How do you help change a world gone mad, full of pollution, war and intolerance? How can you wake up to life and live a happier more fulfilling existence?

Here are some ideas that might get you thinking and moving towards a more 'Hippie Kushi' life:

The Rainbow Family

The Rainbow Family is a loose association of hippie tribes with their roots in the 1960s. Many people all over the world have kept the ideals of hippie living through community, peace, freedom and happiness.

Some of these tribes have permanent camps made up of caravans, tents and makeshift enclosures or they take over disused buildings and squat or alternatively they live in community homes and farms where everyone chips in with the cooking, cleaning and bills. It is often expected that certain rules are followed, such as veganism and political viewpoints.

This kind of living is not for everyone, it's often an outside life and can be dirty and hand to mouth. But for others it's paradise.

Ashrams, Monasteries and Temples

Some find peace and happiness through Eastern religions, meditation and retreats. We have all seen the happy faces of the Hare Krishna followers singing and dancing along the streets of our cities. Seeing these happy shaven-headed disciples chanting 'Hare Krishna Hare Rama' as they hand out books about their own vision of happiness, always makes me smile and I must admit, even from childhood I have felt the draw of joining their ranks and singing along with them.

India has many Hindu Ashrams (spiritual retreats) where people from all over the world can come and stay for extended periods, listening to wise gurus and embracing their inner spirituality, through meditation and quiet contemplation. Small donations are expected as well as help with chores around the complex. One such retreat is Auroville in Southern India (www.auroville.org).

Many in the West have also embraced Buddhism and regularly attend temples in their hometowns to listen to spiritual leaders and to meditate. For others, travelling abroad and actually becoming a monk in places like Thailand, Tibet and Vietnam is the only way they can truly find inner peace.

Native Villages

In 2004 I spent over a year in the Gambia, Africa. I worked as a teacher in a remote tribal village. The village kept livestock, grew vegetables and was completely self-sufficient. Despite its poverty and lack of running water and electricity, the people were happy and I loved the way of life. I was only there a short time but I did meet people from all over the world that had chosen to live there fulltime and were living a happy and fulfilling life because of the collective, community ideal. If you are accepted by the village people through your deeds and community spirit, you can live a life that is the ultimate change of pace and cultural experience.

Eel Pie Island, London

Eel Pie Island is a private island on the Thames in Twickenham not far from where I live in Hampton. It's home to a mix of new-age hippies, inventors, bohemians, artists and boat builders.

In the 1960s it was known for the Eel Pie Hotel, a music venue that attracted David Bowie, Pink Floyd and the Rolling Stones. It is a happy diverse community of individuals living the alternative lifestyle dream.

Finca Bellavista

Finca Bellavista is to be found in the beautiful Costa Rican rainforest. It is a network of hand-built tree houses and is home to an eco-community. All energy used is generated by solar systems. Most food is grown on-site and all of the structures have been built to interfere as little as possible with the natural plant and animal life around it. The treehouses are connected by aerial walkways and zip-lines and if you don't want to live there full-time you can rent them for a retreat.

Christiana – Copenhagen, Denmark

I once visited this 84-acre 'town' in Copenhagen which was founded in 1971 by a group of anarchic squatters and artists. It was originally an abandoned military base but is now described as a 'free zone'.

Once again this is all about community living. The town is best known for 'Pusher Street' a cobbled lane where an estimated $150 million of cannabis sales are made each year, so the odd police raid is inevitable as cannabis use is illegal in Denmark.

Initially dismissed by most as a hippie fad, 40 years on it's one of the longest-lasting communes in history.

Goa Hippie Community, Arambol and Anjuna, India

I couldn't end this part of the chapter without mentioning my beloved Goa, could I?

There is a hippie community still thriving in Goa India, especially around the areas of Arambol and Anjuna. Since the 1960s hippies have travelled the hippie trail to India and settled in Goa. To this day there are scattered hippie communities in these areas living the dream. It's not easy – many create and sell trinkets like jewellery and crafts in the markets to survive, often getting arrested by the police as westerners are not permitted to legally sell at these markets. Others are buskers and play music at venues like the day and night markets. They live in hand-made huts and tree houses along the beaches and the surrounding areas. The community is vibrant and there are many hippie bars, live music venues and trance parties.

Goa is my chosen destination for Waking Up to Life; I hope you find yours.

Hippie Kushi!

*

Community Living, Co-operative Living: Why Do Some Choose This Way of Life and Could It Be for You?

I now want to explore a completely different way of living and whether you might consider a complete change in lifestyle. This way of life is certainly not for everyone – for some, it would be their idea of hell but for others, it would be their idea of a total and perfect heaven.

"A commune (the French word appearing in the twelfth century from Medieval Latin communia, meaning a large gathering of people sharing a common life; from Latin communis, things held in common) is an intentional community of people living together, sharing common interests, often having common values and beliefs, as well as shared property, possessions, resources, and, in some communes, work, income or assets. In addition to the communal economy, consensus decision-making, non-hierarchical structures and ecological living have become important core principles for many communes. There are many contemporary intentional communities all over the world, a list of which can be found at the Fellowship for Intentional Community (FIC)."
Source: Wikipedia

Europe's Historical Role in Housing Cooperatives

"The cooperative housing movement began in Europe in the nineteenth century, primarily in Great Britain and France, as a means to provide affordable housing for persons whose other choices might be rental of a tenement flat from a landlord that controlled the premises much like a king controls his kingdom. Cooperatives also provided a solution to housing shortages that arose when industrial development attracted people into the cities and targeted as working-class families who could not afford to purchase a home. They offered sound shelter at affordable prices relying on self-help efforts of members to reduce costs." **Source: nationalcooperativelawcenter.com**

Co-operative living became especially popular during the time of the hippie movement in America in the 1960s. At this time in my life, I find this idea very attractive but I also have my doubts. The idea of living as part of a new age community somewhere in a beautiful part of the British countryside, living with like-minded people, living off the land, cooking together, socialising together, looking after chickens and goats and exploring spirituality and creativity; whilst at the same time looking out for each other is a lovely concept. But for me, I think I would be happier having more of my own space. When you cook together and eat together and do everything else as a collective, it could get a bit all-consuming.

This is why my canal boat dream suites my personality better; you are part of a close-knit community that lives out of each other's pockets, but if you want your own space, you just turn on the ignition, undo your mooring ropes and take yourself away for a while.

It all depends on your personality and your needs; some people love to be around others 24/7.

A great website for finding these communities is the Diggers and Dreamers website. Here is a typical advert:

Diggers & Dreamers THE GUIDE TO COMMUNAL LIVING IN BRITAIN

Earth Heart

"Earth Heart Housing Co-operative is a co-housing community in a very quiet and beautiful part of rural Derbyshire, five miles outside Ashbourne and close to the Peak District National Park. Earth Heart owns the freehold of the Grade II listed converted farmhouse and barns. The east wing of the barns is partially converted to create a communal hall for meetings and gatherings, as well as workshop space and storage. We are as ecological as we can manage/afford, having a communal wood pellet boiler for heating, a reed bed waste-water treatment system and using a green electricity company.

The surrounding 21 acres of organic land is managed primarily for nature conservation. There is a large parkland running down to Henmore Brook with a moat (an English Heritage scheduled ancient monument) and other small pastures (grazed with a local organic farmer's sheep and cows). There is a secluded woodland with a tree circle, a community orchard and allotments with vegetables, fruit and herbs. There is a willow labyrinth and dome, a composting toilet and solar shower dome. Members of the community own 900+ year leases on the eight individual homes and each home has private use of a small garden. We set up in 1997 around principles of natural parenting and home-education. We aim for a diverse group of people of a variety of ages, including singles, couples and families with children, with home-owning members as well as tenants and non-member lodgers. Most people are employed off-site but some are based from home. We have the advantage of being able to enjoy our independent lives with privacy when we want it, whilst also living within a mutually supportive and sociable community.

We have community work days and business meetings once a month and occasional 'sharing' meetings. Important decisions are taken by consensus and general management is carried out by land, maintenance, finance and administration teams. We have a minimum co-op work requirement for every resident with an expectation of everyone doing a fair share and we understand that nothing gets done unless we all contribute. We expect people to participate regularly in co-op meetings but they are not compulsory.

We are not open to the public but offer guided walks and workshops for groups of six people or more. We also host and run various camps during the spring and summer and are happy to consider hosting new groups for camps. Opportunities arise from time to time to buy, rent or lodge here. If you are interested in visiting with a view to going on our waiting list, do email us for further details. There are currently two properties for sale and a room to rent, see 'Places Needing Members'.

Interested in joining Earth Heart Housing Coop? There are currently two properties for sale – THE OLD STABLES, and THE MOAT HOUSE, AND A ROOM TO RENT

*

RENT A ROOM – Single person required to share top floor flat of listed building farmhouse. Own room plus use of living room/kitchen, bathroom and garden. Vegetarian, non-smoker preferred. Resident dog and cat so sorry no more pets. Own transport necessary. £100 per week all bills included."

In this advert, you can see many reasons why this kind of living is appealing to people who strive for this kind of existence.

More on Community Living

Source: www.thegoodtrade.com

Cohousing is not just house sharing, it is a way of life, a passion for collective living. It is a community of likeminded people all working together for mutual benefit.

Many or even most have a strong focus on sustainability. Preserving open natural spaces, renewable energy projects, growing your own vegetables and in doing so, being stewards for the land and environment you are responsible for.

Financing the project is a collective endeavour. Everyone helps out both financially and physically when things need building, mending or sustaining.
Source: www.thegoodtrade.com

Here is just one example of a co-op housing community in the UK, care of an article from the Independent:

Benches, Housing Co-Operative, Rental, Six Residents

"Dodgy landlords, leaking roofs, ever-increasing rent and isolated lives. Sound familiar? It did to us..."

Lloyd Russell-Moyle, 25, from Sussex, an original member of the co-operative, says that they hoped to provide a "safety net" for young people when they set up the co-operative. Members pay an average of £40 rent a week to the landlord and £15 to cover communal activities, some of which goes towards a savings fund, out of which they hope to purchase their own house in the coming months. Source: Sarah Morrison – **www.independent.co.uk**

For more info see: radicalroutes.org.uk/list-of-members/housing-co-ops/branches.html

If living in a housing cooperative isn't for you, perhaps living full time in a campervan might tickle your fancy:

Full-Time Campervan Living

The world is a beautiful place and full of natural wonders – its beautiful sights are ready for exploring. How wonderful it is to be near to nature, near to a forest or a lake, a mountain or a beach? I have always had the wanderlust and have travelled extensively.

Travelling often means a flight on a plane to get me to my destination, or sometimes a train ride, a voyage on a boat or a bus trip; reaching my destination is sometimes a relief (especially when flying) but I have to admit I am one of those strange people who enjoy the journey just as much as the destination.

So, what a wonderful thing it would be to have your home with you when you travel, to stop off where ever you want and put the kettle on while admiring the view. Imagine carrying your home on your back like some multi-coloured fast-moving tortoise. Could you consider full-time campervan living?

All over the world thousands of people with a similar mind-set and outlook on life are living in a van, motorhome or campervan full time. They travel the roads and highways of the planet like a band of colourful nomadic new age gipsy's; constantly on the move, exploring our beautiful country, meeting new people, trying out new things and having adventures.

"Living in a van is a bit like camping. You can access all sorts of beautiful places whilst living close to nature and having no ties to one fixed location. But it's a lot more comfortable than camping. You have everything with you. You have your books, music, gas and electricity. You can be warm and dry and have proper cooked meals. Everything you need. And you can drive away any time you like. You have the comfort of a house and the benefits of no house. But you do have a home, and the world is your garden." **How to Live in a Van and Travel – Mike Hudson**

I wrote earlier about my long-term goal of living on a canal boat on the beautiful waterways of this country. Close to the wildlife, the water, to nature and to the extraordinary people that live on the canals as part of the canal boat community.

I will never let go of that dream. But canal boats range in cost from about £14000 to £140,000 and cost a lot to maintain, let alone the taxes, licences and insurance and mooring costs.

I recently came into some money and my first reaction was to start on the boat buying ladder. You see in order for me to buy a canal boat, I would first have to make a lot of sacrifices, cut costs massively, leave my flat and live somewhere a fraction of the price in order to save the money needed for the canal boat.

My first instinct after receiving the windfall pay out was to buy a small cruiser (boat) to live on. Many new canal boat owners do this in order to buy a better canal boat later.

After going to see a number of boats I realised that for the money I had, I would be lucky to get a rundown second-hand cruiser the size of a bathtub (slight exaggeration). Winter is coming, my health is not great (I have just recovered from a chest infection), I would feel claustrophobic and unhappy; it was a step too far, and all this at the top of my budget at around £8000 for a 25 ft. cruiser.

Another thing I have considered over the years as an alternative to a small boat is a campervan. This would also allow me to cut costs and save up for my canal boat.

Recently at the Whirl-y-Fayre festival I got talking to campervan owners; both long-term van dwellers and those who use them occasionally for recreation; I was totally won over to the merits of this idea.

This sort of life is totally for me – the open road, the nomadic hippie existence, and the freedom of the lifestyle.

For a start, a second-hand motorhome cost on average £2000 to £3000 from places like Facebook Marketplace. They are warmer, have more room and better facilities than a small cruising boat. I am convinced this is the answer.

I have decided after a lot of research to move in this direction and have now signed up to a driving school in Hampton. Yes, you heard me right. Because you see, as stated previously, the first problem is, I have never driven – I cannot drive. I have always wanted to but have never got around to it. I now have my provisional licence and lessons start in two weeks.

So, let's explore this subject in more detail. Let's take a look at the phenomenon of long term live-aboard campervan life.

First, Let's Look at Why Some Choose This Life

If you are like me, you have never conformed to regular life; you are a free soul. For many working a nine to five office job, paying a mortgage and settling down in suburbia just isn't for them.

Some of us strive for freedom – the freedom to travel, to have the potential to wake up next to a beautiful German lake or on top of a mountain in Morocco; to eat breakfast overlooking the Scottish Highlands or meeting friends at a hippie housing collective in Wales; all this just by jumping in our campervan and driving off.

Our home on wheels gives us the freedom to visit friends anywhere in the country, to attend festivals and gatherings; the freedom of the road matches our free-spirit mind-set.

Mike Hudson on life before becoming a full-time campervan nomad:

"Over winter I'd drive to work in the dark, sit in the office with no windows all day and drive myself home in the dark. This is what many people do, but thinking about it now, it seems crazy. When I look back at photos of myself from the last year of that job, I don't look healthy. My face is pale and my eyes are like dark grey circles." **How to Live in a Van and Travel – Mike Hudson**

Now Let's Look at the Merits of This Lifestyle:

Certainly, it costs a lot less than renting a flat; your outgoings are a fraction of what they would be – now that you are not paying for council tax, bills and all the other materialistic things you would normally surround yourself with.

Of course, this takes sacrifice, to live this life you need to downsize massively, live a simpler life; which to me sounds wonderful.

"LIVE FOR LESS; House living costs take up a considerable amount of most people's earnings. A van bypasses all of that and lets you save the extra money per month which can help you get out of debt, save up, start a business or just buy yourself some time. In this way a van can give you a huge leg up. But it's not just rent. A van can save you a lot of money on hostels and hotels when travelling." **How to Live in a Van and Travel – Mike Hudson**

There are of course costs involved – van upkeep, camping site fees (if you fancy having some mains electricity, hot water and Wi-Fi), petrol and car insurance etc. but this is tiny compared to the cost of renting a property.

Another reason for living full time in a campervan is that they can be much roomier than say, a small cruiser boat. The good ones have a toilet (A cassette toilet needs emptying at camping sites), a shower room, a fridge, oven, stove, sink, heating, bed or beds, a table and chairs and often an awning to provide more space outside of the vehicle. It really is like a mini home on wheels.

I think you need to have a bit of the gipsy in you to live this lifestyle but it does have its plus sides.

"TRAVEL: Travelling in a van is not like normal travelling where you go from point to point, checking in at hostels or hotels on the way and sticking very much to the travel grid. Having a van gives you access to everywhere and allows you to see places you probably wouldn't see otherwise. You experience all the things in between and get a taste of the whole country. And because you have your home on your back, you can pull up in some amazing spot and live there without being bound by check-in times." **How to Live in a Van and Travel – Mike Hudson**

Negatives:

Having no postal address; you would need to set up a post office account somewhere to pick up your mail (or you could use a relative's address or a friend).

Finding a GP when you are on the move; there are ways around this; use a relative or friends address when you register.

The issue of emptying a full to the brim toilet is another difficulty (if you can find somewhere to empty it).

Parking: can also be a tricky business. You are not legally allowed to just park on the street and sleep. Van dwellers I have spoken to say country lanes are OK if you are out of sight (this is much easier and more accepted in Europe). Many farms will let you stop on their land as long as you ask first. Use Facebook to find local hippie communes and camps and ask if you can stop there for a few nights and of course camping sites are relatively cheap to park up at and they often have good facilities; just get yourself a good AA camping site guide.

But How Do You Pay Your Way if You Are on the Move?

There are many ways you can pay for such a life. A couple I spoke to, at Whirl-y-Fayre worked for an events company (festivals, fayres and horticultural events) working the bars and stewarding. This tends to be more of a summer thing but anyone who does bar work knows there is always bar work to be had somewhere (even in winter) that will pay your way.

Bloggers do OK as long as they have the readers. Advertising payments can keep you comfortably on top of things as long as you can live cheaply.

Other types of internet-based work are good just as long as your employer is happy for you to work from home (or van).

Or, as I am planning to do, you could anchor yourself to a specific area at first and work somewhere for three or four days a week. Then you can travel on the other days. Although this can initially limit your ability to travel extensively, you still have the freedom to develop your own projects (in my case my street market/online hippie clothing and jewellery store, my art and my writing) which over time, once successful, can replace the job that ties you to that specific area (always the practical one Stephen) and you still have the freedom and low cost of living in a campervan.

It makes me smile to think of a life travelling around the UK and Europe in a hippiefied campervan; working in local pubs, at festivals and possibly even fruit picking on farms; whilst running my business, keeping up my blog, making my art and writing my next book.

"**FESTIVALS:** Having a van is a nice way to do festivals. It's difficult to go back to a cold, damp tent after having the luxury of a van with full living facilities. Just being able to get up in the morning and make a coffee without getting dressed to queue at a stall makes it worth it." **How to Live in a Van and Travel – Mike Hudson**

Visiting friends around the country and staying at hippie coops and communes; enjoying great festivals all over Europe. All the time building up your own projects and business, so, eventually you have total freedom and hippie happiness; and for me, eventually saving up enough to buy that canal boat.

"**TAKE A STEP BACK:** We're constantly being told what to do and how to live, how to look and what to buy. It makes life stressful. Being able to take a step back and distance yourself from all of this can be invaluable opportunity, and a van lets you do it." **How to Live in a Van and Travel – Mike Hudson**

Interior:

Express yourself – your campervan will come with all the facilities you need (if not, you can install them yourself) but it will need a bit of work to make it truly yours; it's all about individuality. Make your home your palace with decorations and upholstery; pimp it up and hippiefy your world.

"**ESCAPE THE WINTER**: I don't know about you but I become like a zombie during the winter, in those three months of darkness. Apart from affecting the regulation of melatonin in the brain, it also makes us deficient in vitamin D, which is not cool. But with a van you can go south for the winter and be a 'snowbird'. This has changed everything for me. I'm so much better and happier when the sky is bright. It's probably why thousands of other people in Europe and the US also do this." **How to Live in a Van and Travel – Mike Hudson**

Hmm, six weeks in Goa and the rest of the winter travelling in my campervan around the South of France, Spain and Portugal; that's a really hard decision to make. I suppose I could do it… of course, I could do it!!!

"I don't want to be the one thing for the rest of my life. I don't want to pick something from life's set-menu and be labelled as one single job title forever. I want to be loads of things. I want my life to be full of chapters, not blurred memories of a nine-to-five routine. And I don't want the chapters to be rungs on a career ladder. I want to make my own ladder, putting the rungs in as I go along. And I don't want the ladder to go in a straight line." **How to Live in a Van and Travel – Mike Hudson**

It seems to me that living full time in a campervan is a good life and a potentially a mind-expanding experience. You might not want to do it forever (although some do) but it would certainly be a memorable part of your life and one that could help you save up for your dreams while living an incredible nomadic lifestyle.

And once you are ready for your next chapter (for me, my canal boat) you know you will take with you some amazing memories.

The book I have quoted from in this chapter is an excellent guide for anyone wanting to take up the campervan life: HOW TO LIVE IN A VAN AND TRAVEL – MIKE HUDSON – Bluedog Books

Mike Hudson

Biography

"From the UK, I live in a van that I made into my full-time home – this is where I write from. My van-home has let me live nomadically, all over Europe, for the past three years. Whoa, I've had an incredible time and I'm lucky I've been able to create this life of freedom for myself. I want to show you how I've done it. See vandogtraveller.com – all about living free and travelling and just enjoying life. I've done two books now. I hope they help you."

Perhaps the last two options seem a bit extreme for you and you need a bit more comfort; how about living on a canal boat?

Living on a Canal Boat; Canal Boat Communities

If you have ever considered a life on the water, surrounded by nature and living amongst a unique canal boat community, here is a little insight into this wonderful nomadic way of living.

I have dreamt most of my life of living on the water in a funky canal boat, painted hippie style on the outside with an interior that suits my personality.

I would probably take up a permanent mooring, which can seem expensive to some but when you compare it to renting a property; it's not really expensive at all. A mooring, often with an electricity and water supply can cost between £1500 and £8000 a year. It gives you security (these permanent moorings are often gated and locked with access only for boat owners), you can go away and travel for months knowing your boat is safe and secure. If you think that a one-bedroom flat in London is around £1000 to £1600 a month, even the highest mooring costs of £8000 a year is a fraction of that. Also, I personally would only use a permanent mooring as a home base, more often than not travelling up and down this beautiful country's canal system. Mooring up when I see somewhere that tickles my fancy and enjoying getting to know the oddball eccentric community of boat people that create the canal boat sub-culture.

But is this the dream life it's made out to be?

I love boats and I love water, I was born in Brighton by the sea and have always felt a connection to the water. I now live in Hampton on the Surrey border, right by the river Thames. It's a beautiful area and there are loads of canal boats. I love to sit and watch them from the riverbank on a summer's day.

Living on a boat would give me the peace, freedom and happiness I am looking for. In order to decide if this is the right choice for me (and you), you need to learn as much as possible about living on and running a canal boat as well as the ways of the water (the laws, the licences and the etiquette). My personal plan is to first volunteer with a canal boat charity called the Hillingdon Narrowboats Association, a charity that provides day and weekend trips out on the canals for children. Volunteers help with keeping the boats in tip-top condition and also with the trips with the kids.

hillingdon-narrowboats.org.uk. In exchange, you get to learn everything 'canal boat', the laws around boating as set out by the Canals and Rivers Trust, boat maintenance, steering and operating the boat, mooring up, operating locks, filling the water tanks and fuelling the engine as well as the more unpleasant duties such as emptying the waste tank.

With the money I would save by living in a campervan for two years, I could be well on my way towards getting my canal boat and fulfilling my life-long dream.

But a warning: one thing you should always do before purchasing your canal boat (if you don't intend to be a continuous cruiser) is to secure a mooring first; they are hard to find and often have long waiting lists.

What will you do when you have your boat?

For me, I would spend the summer months in the UK living on my boat, exploring this country's many canals and using my boat as a base to run my small business. And in the winter month's I would travel to my beloved Goa in India on my continuing search for peace, freedom and happiness.

Doesn't sound like a bad plan, does it? But what are the realities of my dream? There are a lot of things to think about before taking the leap – below is a great article I came across about canal boat living:

The Pros and Cons of Living Afloat

www.waterways.org.uk

"During much of my seven years living on a narrowboat, I travelled around a lot and religiously moved the boat every two weeks. For a lot of this time, I was working as a secretarial 'temp' so was able to move from town to town and pick up work anywhere. As well as wanting to comply with the rules, moving every two weeks was necessary for practical reasons, being an opportunity to fill the water tank and visit a boatyard to get the toilet pumped out and occasionally fill up with diesel and get gas bottles replaced."

The Pros and Cons of Living Afloat *www.waterways.org.uk*

There are definitely pros and cons worth thinking about before jumping in and buying a canal boat. I hope this information has answered some questions and laid out the realities of this lifestyle. If I have inspired those thinking of making this move of living on a boat, then I wish you all the best in this endeavour.

So there we are a few alternative lifestyles to consider. Do you think an alternative lifestyle is for you? Don't let any fears or the advice of others or moving out of your comfort zone stop you. If your life is dull, change it! If you dream of travelling the world, do it! If you want to live on a canal boat or in a hippiefied motorhome, go for it! Life is meant for living: what's holding you back?

An alternative lifestyle is not for everyone but whichever way you choose to live your life, remember this; in order to achieve complete freedom and hippie happiness you simply have to take the leap.

*

Chapter Twelve
My Blog

In 2017 I started my own blog as way of an outlet for my feelings around becoming a bit stuck in life. I toyed with many titles and subject matters and initially it was to be about moving on from a full-stop life. This was before my epiphany in Goa and the avalanche of life change I experienced after that fateful trip. The fledgling blog did have the underlying hippie theme to it as this was something I had always related too, but my initial set up was a cheap WordPress program and my posts on it held very little substance.

Since my trip to Goa, I felt fired up, I changed the blog name from 'Releasing my inner hippie' (urk) to Hippie Kushi Waking Up to Life, after looking up the Hindu word for happiness (I now wanted the blog to be all about finding a collective hippie happiness and the success of my Facebook community based around this subject proves this was a wise choice).

In the beginning I still had the free cheap and nasty template but the substance of my blog improved and a few people started paying attention to it and commenting positively and I gained a few followers.

Later in this process a work friend told me about a free online blogging boot camp run by a great guy called James and after a bit of investigation I quickly signed up. The boot camp taught us how to build a good professional blog site and what that site needed in way of extras and apps and links. Also how we could grow our reader base by using multiple social media sites and advertising our blogs. But most importantly it taught us how to think about what it was we were writing about and who our audience was.

I had never been on social media before and over the course of the boot camp I set up accounts on Pinterest, Instagram, Facebook, Twitter and YouTube. The focus of my blog was to be about not being boring when you are older and the search for hippie happiness, as well as vagabonding travel and alternative lifestyles.

I would create a pin poster for each post I wrote and put it onto Pinterest with a link to my blog – this accelerated my readership to the 100s. I then started putting photos and videos (via YouTube) and links on Instagram and also linked a discussion on Twitter; now my readership rose up to the 1000s.

The biggest promotion tool though has been Facebook. I joined the Whirl-y-Gig Facebook page, multiple traveller/backpacker groups, Goa hippie group pages, Whirl-y-Fayre, another festival group as well as having my own personal page and my specially created group page called Hippie Kushi Waking Up to Life (which is now super popular).

Every time I wrote a post, I put it onto these Facebook pages with a link to the blog. I have now upgraded and modernised my blog and it looks great. Three years on and my readership is over 10000 a month, even to the point where most people at Whirl-y-Gig tend to call me 'Hippie Kushi' rather than Stephen; which is fun.

I love writing it – it's a great catharsis and outlet for me and readers seem to enjoy it too. So here are a few examples of some of the posts I have written on hippiekushiwakinguptolife.com:

HIPPIE KUSHI WAKING UP TO LIFE
Alternative Lifestyles * Vagabonding Travel * Searching for Hippie Happiness

FOLLOWING MY DREAMS: A NEW FOCUS

I'm Not Religious, I'm Spiritual

Have You Ever Said This? I Have, What Does That Even Mean?
Blog Post MAY 17th 2018

I have always felt uncomfortable using the term 'God'. What does that even mean to me? A Christian upbringing at a church school, with boring church services every day and visions of a mythical white-bearded man in the sky.

What I have really felt during my life is something quite different, a different idea of spirituality. I have always felt that God was something different, not a man but more of an energy source all around us. This energy source or Brahman as I prefer to call it is everything. Brahman is in the trees, the plants, the animals and the sea, the sunshine, the moon, the planets, the stars, the people and all the things we see and cannot see. It is love, it is hate, it is war and it is peace.

As I have grown older, I feel I have taken comfort in my search for happiness through spirituality. During my visits to India, I have often felt this power of light through the atmosphere of joy within its people but there is also something in the air. You come away feeling different.

The Indian people, both Buddhists and Hindus believe in reincarnation, as do I. I believe we are reborn time and time again and it is through our deeds that our next incarnation is chosen. The Hindus call this Karma.

Many people who search out spiritual peace and enlightenment as an alternative lifestyle to the unhappy one they have been living, often turn to Eastern Spirituality. Many westerners practice Buddhism and meditate regularly as well as attending Buddhist temples. Some have chosen to join the Hare Krishna groups throughout the world, a type of Hinduism. These colourful happy souls can be seen chanting and singing up and down our high streets handing out books about this beautiful religion.

The closest I have found to the kind of spiritual beliefs I believe in is that of Hinduism. Their idea of god is exactly the same as mine. But you may be saying 'hold on, the Hindu faith has thousands of gods' but these gods are all manifestations of the one 'light' that is Brahman.

If you are looking for something different, something spiritual, here is an outline of two Eastern religions, or spiritual paths you may wish to explore further:

Buddhism

Buddhism began in India 2,500 years ago and remains the dominant world religion in the East. There are over 360 million followers of Buddhism worldwide and over a million American Buddhists today. Buddhist concepts have also been influential on western culture in general, particularly in the areas of meditation and nonviolence.

Buddhism is based on the teachings of a Nepali prince named Siddharta Gautama who lived around 500 BCE. According to Buddhist tradition, the sheltered young prince was shocked by the suffering he saw outside his palace walls, so he left his life of luxury to seek answers. Eventually, he succeeded, becoming the Buddha – the 'Enlightened One'. He spent the remaining 45 years of his life teaching the dharma (the path to liberation from suffering) and establishing the sangha (a community of monks).

Over its long history, Buddhism has taken a wide variety of forms. Some emphasise rituals and the worship of deities, while others completely reject rituals and gods in favour of pure meditation. Yet all forms of Buddhism share a respect for the teachings of the Buddha and the goal of ending suffering and the cycle of rebirth.

Theravada Buddhism, prominent in Southeast Asia, is atheistic and philosophical in nature and focuses on the monastic life and meditation as a means to liberation. Mahayana Buddhism, prominent in China and Japan, incorporates several deities, celestial beings, and other traditional religious elements. In Mahayana, the path to liberation may include religious ritual, devotion, meditation, or a combination of these elements. Zen, Nichiren, Tendai, and Pure Land are the major forms of Mahayana Buddhism.

Hinduism

There are an estimated one billion Hindus worldwide, making Hinduism the third-largest religion after Christianity and Islam. About 80% of India's population regard themselves as Hindus and 30 million more Hindus live outside of India.

Hinduism has no founder or date of origin. The authors and dates of most Hindu sacred texts are unknown, although the oldest texts (the Vedas) are estimated to date from as early as 1500 BCE. Scholars describe Hinduism as the product of religious development in India that spans nearly 4,000 years, making it perhaps the oldest surviving world religion.

The broad term "Hinduism" encompasses a wide variety of traditions, which are closely related and share common themes but do not constitute a unified set of beliefs or practices. Hinduism is not a homogeneous, organised system. Many Hindus are devoted followers of Shiva or Vishnu, whom they regard as the only true God, while others look inward to the divine Self (atman). But most recognise the existence of Brahman, the unifying principle and Supreme Reality behind all that is.

Most Hindus respect the authority of the Vedas (the oldest sacred texts) and the Brahmans (the priestly class), but some reject one of both of these authorities. Hindu religious life might take the form of devotion to God or gods, the duties of family life, or concentrated meditation. Given all this diversity, it is important to take care when generalising about 'Hinduism' or 'Hindu beliefs'.

The first sacred writings of Hinduism, which date to about 1500-1200 BCE, were primarily concerned with the ritual sacrifices associated with numerous gods who represented forces of nature. A more philosophical focus began to develop around 700 BCE, with the Upanishads and development of the Vedanta philosophy. Around 500 BCE, several new belief systems sprouted from Hinduism, most significantly Buddhism and Jainism.

In the twentieth century, Hinduism began to gain popularity in the West. Its different worldview and its tolerance for diversity in belief made it an attractive alternative to traditional Western religion. Although there are relatively few western converts to Hinduism specifically, Hindu thought has influenced the West indirectly by way of religious movements like Hare Krishna and New Age, and even more so through the incorporation of Indian beliefs and practices (such as the chakra system and yoga) into health and spirituality.

For me spirituality is all about happiness, all about feeling peaceful and enlightened; it's all about Hippie Kushi Waking Up to Life.

I have started reading a wonderful book called Hero for High Times by Ian Marchant, which has a wonderful quote that sums up not only my blog but spirituality in general and that Hippie Kushi feeling:

"The Freaks thought the world was broken, and they might have found a new way of mending it. They wanted freedom, and happiness, and a world in which people could be themselves, which meant that there would be no war, no famine and no disease. The freaks thought that in order to make this happen, everyone and everything needed to change. And to change everything, the freaks were going to teach the world to play. The freaks wanted everybody to look at

everything in a new way. A new way which allows people to live their lives how they choose, no matter what anybody else thinks or says. A way where we can dance and sing and play all day. A way where love is the most powerful force in the universe, and where people see that the world is a wonderful, magical place."
Hero for High Times by Ian Marchant

*

A Hippie Guide to Goa

Blog Post JUNE 3rd 2018

"Before Goa became a commercialised tourist destination, it was known for its 'hippie culture'.

Explaining how and why the cultural movement started in Goa, Prateek Dham in a piece for Tripoto writes:

1970s was the time when the hippies had taken fully-grown wings and started migrating to freer pastures in order to attain what they were eternally looking for – salvation."

And Goa proved to be just the right place for them.

"Not only were Goans accommodating of all cultures, the Indian government also did not oppose the influx because it was contributing to the local economy in an otherwise turbulent economic time in the country," he adds. (Exert taken from The News Minute – Friday, September 2nd 2016)

There is one reason above all others why I fell in love with Goa the first time I went there, and that is the colourful hippie scene that still flourishes there after all these years. When I first visited Goa, I found the place to be not only beautiful and full of character but also alive with a hippie vibe that is exciting and vibrant.

So for those of you that want to visit Goa in search of this Hippie Kushi vibe here is the rundown on where to go, what to do and a few suggestions on the music soundtrack you may wish to take with you.

Arambol

"Goa is one of the places in the world where hippie culture still heavily permeates society at large as a way of life. The first hippies came to Goa during the end of the last century. They stayed because of Anjuna, Baga and Vagator beaches. The reason that Goa attracted young hippies was that they were enthralled by its tropics, an atmosphere of spirituality and isolated nature. This came as a huge contrast to the conservatism of old Europe. What makes Goa so distinctive, not only in India but abroad, is the fact that hippie culture is very pertinent." **Source: hippie-inheels.com**

So where are most of Goa's hippies?

"The hippies who live in Goa are situated mainly in north Goa, around the beaches of Arambol, Ashvem and Morjim. Yoga, meditation, running and other outdoor activities make up the majority of their day. People come to Goa to experience an idealistic way of life, where urban and industrial commitments don't govern citizen attitudes. While masses of hippies have left Goa, they leave behind their yester-year ideals. They also leave strong cultural influences, religious identity, and a spirit that ignited change in the first place."

Source: theplaidzebra.com

Drum Circle and Market

"Drums circles happen every evening at the far end of the beach. Locals, expats and travellers meet here to play drums as the sun goes down and everyone dances together. The atmosphere is amazing – everyone dancing for the sheer love of dancing. There are children running all around. It's amazing to see people from all over the world coming together each evening to make music. Next to the drumming circle is a small market where expats sell handmade jewellery and Mr Cookie from Cookie Waller sells cookies!" **Source: hippie-inheels.com**

Arambol is for me the most authentic place to feel that hippie vibe. To sit on the beach and watch as the sun goes down, listening to hippies playing all kinds of instruments while others dance with their feet in the surf; for me, its paradise.

Anjuna

When you enter Anjuna beach, your Tuk Tuk will drop you at the top of a red-tinged sandy winding road that cuts through a local market. The market sells all kinds of hippie and Indian regalia and it's where I purchased the stuff to do up my bedroom back in the UK.

After the market, there are several restaurants and bars overlooking the ocean. These bars have live new age music in the evening, drawing in an eclectic hippie crowd.

Anjuna Live Music

Also situated here are different kinds of budget accommodation, sometimes in local homes. These attract mainly new age hippie types.

After this, you come out onto Anjuna beach, home of hippie bars, trance clubs, beach shacks and low-cost cabins for rent with air conditioning and with pleasant interiors.

There is a nice hippie community here that often frequent the bars and can be seen dancing all night at one of the many trance parties.

Another draw for Anjuna is the Wednesday Day Market:

This market is definitely a great place to feel the hippie vibe. There are lots of older hippies here enjoying the colourful stalls alongside their younger new age counterparts. The stalls sell everything from jewellery, Hindu statues, tie-dyed trousers and incense sticks as well as some great food. Many of the hippies that live full time in Goa sell their homemade crafts here but they always have to have one eye out for the police as foreigners are not legally allowed to work there.

After the market stalls close the bars and clubs inside the market come alive. Anjuna is an exciting and fun place to find peace, love and harmony.

Arpora Night Market

"The night market in Arpora, also known as The Saturday Night Market or Ingos Saturday Nite Bazaar is the largest shopping and entertainment event, which reflects the cosmopolitan and distinctive culture of Goa state in the best way." **Source: www.goavilla.co.uk/goa**

The atmosphere is incredible and is most definitely hippie heaven.

Live Music at the Night Market

"As you can see from the name, the market takes place on Saturdays. This event happens only during the high tourist season on a large fenced area between the Arpora and Anjuna city resorts. The first season night market is usually arranged before the New Year, while the last one is organized at the end of April (the business hours: from 4:00 p.m. till 11:00 p.m.)."

"The Saturday Night Market in Arpora is a must for sightseeing which every tourist should visit while travelling to Goa. On Saturday evenings the entertainment spots are usually empty because the tourists are flocking to the market. Travel agencies organize special trips to Ingos Saturday Nite Bazaar for tourists who are having their vacations in South Goa."

Hippie Heaven

"The Night Market in Arpora attracts a huge number of local and foreign traders, including European. The range of products includes almost everything you can imagine starting with the penny baubles and trinkets and also with the high-quality branded products and jewellery. Prices are usually too high in comparison to the shops and day markets, but still, you will have a great opportunity to try your skills in the pursuing of dealing prices down to your own desire."

Live Vibes at the Night Market

"The range of food offered in different restaurants here is almost inexhaustible. At the Saturday Night Market in Arpora, you can try amazingly tasty dishes from nearly all international cuisines starting from the local food and Tibetan momo all the way to the German pretzels. All this mixing of people, tastes, smells and colours happens with a backdrop of Goa trance music and lighting effects. The music is played in the restaurants and on the stage in the centre of the market. This scene is specifically built for everyone who really wants to have some fun singing whatever he likes to. There is always a wide empty space around the square, which is usually quickly filled with people dancing. Often big trance parties are held at the Night Market. The entrance into the Ingos Saturday Nite Bazaar is free but is controlled by security guards and with metal detectors. The parking zone is also free, and sometimes it is even difficult to find an empty place on it." **Source: www.goavilla.co.uk/goa**

All of these destinations are great places to meet like-*minded new friends*.

Other great places to go on your hippie trip to Goa:

- Dolphin spotting by boat off Calangute beach
- Crocodile safari
- Dudhsagar Waterfall
- Hindu temples
- The Spice Plantation

Me on my first visit to Goa, still looking pretty square

There are so many more things to do on a Hippie Kushi trip to GOA!!!

Music for Your Travels:

Liquid Sound company – any

Happy Travels
Your comments on 'A Hippie Guide to GOA'

Learn Digital Academy
SEPTEMBER 25th 2018 AT 7:12 A.M.

Thank you for this wondrous post – I am glad I observed this website on GOOGLE. Your blog is very unique and interesting. It makes the reader come back and visit again. Thank you for sharing valuable information nice post, I enjoyed reading this post. Nice Snaps.

Luxury Stays

SEPTEMBER 27th 2018 AT 11:46 A.M.

Travelling will make you more realistic and improve your skills to a whole new level. Travelling to some of the best places makes you more enthusiastic and more knowledgeable person.

*

The Camino de Santiago

Blog Post JUNE 10th 2018

The Pilgrim's Way

"We need sometimes to escape into open solitudes, into aimlessness, into the moral holiday of running some pure hazard, in order to sharpen the edge of life, to taste hardship, and to be compelled to work desperately for a moment no matter what." **GEORGE SANTAYANA – 'THE PHILOSOPHY OF TRAVEL'**

This quote from Santayana beautifully sums up what the Camino de Santiago is all about: finding clarity and a way forward.

The Camino de Santiago is a pilgrimage that has been walked for centuries. Although for many this is a Christian pilgrimage, for thousands of others it is a journey of self-discovery and a way to find clarity and direction in life.

"The pilgrimage to Santiago has never ceased from the time of the discovery of St. James's remains in 812 AD, though there have been years of fewer pilgrims, particularly during European wars."

Time out and a challenge

"Many of us have reached a point in life where we need time to think and time to get away from life as it is. Many times I asked pilgrims why they were on the Camino and the simple answer was just getting away from everything."

For me, the reason I intend to walk the Camino de Santiago next year is as a dividing bridge between the old life I am leaving behind and the new Hippie Kushi life I am now living, with plans of moving onto a boat and travelling five to six months of the year, especially through India. The long walk will allow me to clear my mind and contemplate my future. On top of this, I simply love walking and walking through the beautiful landscapes of Northern France and Spain – it makes the gruelling journey worthwhile. You also meet lots of interesting people along the way.

A great reference to get an idea of what the Camino is like is the fantastic, atmospheric film: 'The Way' starring Martin Sheen:

History and Outline of the Camino:

Source: wikipedia.org

Camino de Santiago

"Is a UNESCO World Heritage Site, its official name: Routes of Santiago de Compostela: Camino Francés and Routes of Northern Spain.

The Camino de Santiago (Latin: Peregrinatio Compostellana, 'Pilgrimage of Compostela'; Galician: O Camiño de Santiago) [1] known in English as the Way of Saint James among other names, is a network of pilgrims' ways serving pilgrimage to the shrine of the apostle Saint James the Great in the cathedral of Santiago de Compostela in Galicia in north-western Spain, where tradition has it that the remains of the saint are buried. Many follow its routes as a form of spiritual path or retreat for their spiritual growth. It is also popular with hiking and cycling enthusiasts and organised tour groups.

The French Way (Camino Francés) and the Routes of Northern Spain are the courses which are listed in the World Heritage List by UNESCO."

The Christian Route

The Cathedral of Santiago de Compostela

"The Way of St. James was one of the most important Christian pilgrimages during the Middle Ages, together with those to Rome and Jerusalem, and a pilgrimage route on which a plenary indulgence could be earned; other major pilgrimage routes include the Via Francigena to Rome and the pilgrimage to Jerusalem.

Legend holds that St. James's remains were carried by boat from Jerusalem to northern Spain, where he was buried in what is now the city of Santiago de Compostela. (The name Santiago is the local Galician evolution of Vulgar Latin Sancti Iacobi, 'Saint James').

The Way can take one of dozens of pilgrimage routes to Santiago de Compostela. Traditionally, as with most pilgrimages, the Way of Saint James began at one's home and ended at the pilgrimage site. However, a few of the routes are considered main ones. During the Middle Ages, the route was highly travelled. However, the Black Death, the Protestant Reformation, and political unrest in sixteenth century Europe led to its decline. By the 1980s, only a few hundred pilgrims per year registered in the pilgrim's office in Santiago. In

October 1987, the route was declared the first European Cultural Route by the Council of Europe; it was also named one of UNESCO's World Heritage Sites. Since the 1980s the route has attracted a growing number of modern-day international pilgrims.

Whenever St. James's Day (July 25th) falls on a Sunday, the cathedral declares a Holy or Jubilee Year. Depending on leap years, Holy Years occur in five, six, and eleven-year intervals. The most recent were 1982, 1993, 1999, 2004, and 2010. The next will be 2021, 2027, and 2032."

History
Monument of the Pilgrims, Burgos
Pre-Christian History

"The main pilgrimage route to Santiago follows an earlier Roman trade route, which continues to the Atlantic coast of Galicia, ending at Cape Finisterre. Although it is known today that Cape Finisterre, Spain's westernmost point, is not the westernmost point of Europe (Cabo da Roca in Portugal is farther west), the fact that the Romans called it Finisterrae (literally the end of the world or Land's End in Latin) indicates that they viewed it as such. At night, the Milky Way overhead seems to point the way, so the route acquired the nickname 'Voie lactée' – the Milky Way in French."

Modern-Day Pilgrimage
The Modern Symbol of the Way

"Today, hundreds of thousands (over 200,000 in 2014) of Christian pilgrims and many others set out each year from their front doorsteps or from popular starting points across Europe, to make their way to Santiago de Compostela. Most (quantify) travel by foot, some by bicycle, and a few (quantify) travel as some of their medieval counterparts did, on horseback or by donkey (for example, the British author and humourist Tim Moore). In addition to those undertaking a religious pilgrimage, many are hikers who walk the route for other reasons: travel, sport, or simply the challenge of weeks of walking in a foreign land. Also, many consider the experience a spiritual adventure to remove themselves from the bustle of modern life. It serves as a retreat for many modern 'pilgrims'."

Routes

A marking in a boardwalk of the Portuguese coastal way: "coastal sands dunes of Póvoa de Varzim."

Here, only a few routes are named. For a complete list of all the routes (traditional and not so much), see: "Camino de Santiago (route descriptions).

A post marking the way:

"Camino Francés, or French Way, is the most popular. The Via Regia is the last portion of the (Camino Francés) (citation needed). Historically, because of the Codex Calixtinus, most pilgrims came from France: typically from Arles, Le Puy, Paris, and Vézelay; some from Saint Gilles. Cluny, site of the celebrated medieval abbey, was another important rallying point for pilgrims and, in 2002, it was integrated into the official European pilgrimage route linking Vézelay and Le Puy.

Camino Primitivo, or Original Way, is the oldest route to Santiago de Compostela, first taken in the ninth century and which begins in Oviedo.

Camino Portugués, or the Portuguese Way, is the second-most-popular route [26] starting at the cathedral in Lisbon (for a total of about 610 km) or at the cathedral in Porto in the north of Portugal (for a total of about 227 km), crossing into Galicia at Valença.

Camino del Norte, or the Northern Way, is also less travelled and starts in the Basque city of Irun on the border with France or sometimes San Sebastián is considered the start of the route. It is far less popular since the route goes up and down a lot (whereas the Camino Frances is mostly flat). The route follows the coast along the Bay of Biscay until it gets close to Santiago. It also does not hit the same number of historic cities and points of interest as the Camino Frances, but is a lot cooler in the summer and most consistently pretty. The route is believed to have been first used by pilgrims to avoid travelling through the territories occupied by the Muslims in the Middle Ages (citation needed).

Most Spanish consider the French border in the Pyrenees the natural starting point. By far the most common starting point on the Camino Francés is Saint-Jean-Pied-de-Port, on the French side of the Pyrenees, with Roncesvalles on the Spanish side also being popular. The distance from Roncesvalles to Santiago de Compostella through León is about 800 km."

Accommodation

St. James's shell, a symbol of the route, on a wall in León, Spain.

"A marker in the pavement indicates the route of the Way of St. James through Navarrete, La Rioja, Spain.

In Spain, France and Portugal, pilgrim's hostels with beds in dormitories dot the common routes, providing overnight accommodation for pilgrims who hold a credential (see below). In Spain, this type of accommodation is called a Refugio or albergue, both of which are similar to youth hostels or hostelries in the French system of gîtes d'étape.

Staying at pilgrims' hostels, known as albergue, usually costs between six and ten euros per night per bed, although a few hostels known as donativos operate on voluntary donations. (Municipal albergues cost six euros, while private albergues generally cost between ten and fifteen euros per night.) Pilgrims are usually limited to one night's accommodation and are expected to leave by eight in the morning to continue their pilgrimage (citation needed).

Hostels may be run by the local parish, the local council, private owners or pilgrims' associations. Occasionally these refugios are located in monasteries, such as the one run by monks in Samos, Spain and the one in Santiago de Compostela.

The final hostel on the route is the famous (according to whom?) Hostal de los Reyes Catolicos, which lies across the plaza from the Cathedral of Santiago de Campostela. It was originally constructed by Ferdinand and Isabel, the Catholic Monarchs. Today it is a luxury five-star Parador hotel, which still (when?) provides free services to a limited number of pilgrims daily."

Credential or Pilgrim's Passport

"St. James pilgrim passport stamps in Spain for the Camino Frances.

St. James pilgrim passport stamps in France on the Via Turonensis (Tours route) for the Chemin de St. Jacques de Compostelle. The World Heritage Sites of the Routes of Santiago de Compostela in France lists the major French towns with stamps.

Most (quantify) pilgrims carry a document called the credential, purchased for a few euros from a Spanish tourist agency, a church or parish house on the route, a refugio, their church back home, or outside of Spain through the national St. James organization of that country. The credential is a pass which gives access to inexpensive, sometimes free, overnight accommodation in refugios along the trail. Also known as the 'pilgrim's passport', the credential is stamped with the official St. James stamp of each town or refugio at which the pilgrim has stayed. It provides pilgrims with a record of where they ate or slept, and serves as proof to the Pilgrim's Office in Santiago that the journey was accomplished according to an official route, and thus that the pilgrim qualifies to receive a compostela (certificate of completion of the pilgrimage).

Most often the stamp can be obtained in the refugio, cathedral, or local church. If the church is closed, the town hall or office of tourism can provide a stamp, as can nearby youth hostels or private St. James addresses. Many of the small restaurants and cafes along the Camino also provide stamps. Outside Spain, the stamp can be associated with something of a ceremony, where the stamper and the pilgrim can share information. As the pilgrimage approaches Santiago, many of the stamps in small towns are self-service due to the greater number of pilgrims, while in the larger towns there are several options to obtain the stamp."

Compostela

"The compostela is a certificate of accomplishment given to pilgrims on completing the Way. To earn the compostela one needs to walk a minimum of 100 km or cycle at least 200 km. In practice, for walkers, the closest convenient point to start is Sarria, as it has good bus and rail connections to other places in Spain. Pilgrims arriving in Santiago de Compostela who have walked at least the last 100 km, or cycled 200 km to get there (as indicated on their credencial), and who state that their motivation was at least partially religious are eligible for the compostela from the Pilgrim's Office in Santiago. At the Pilgrim's Office the credencial is examined for stamps and dates, and the pilgrim is asked to state whether the motivation in traveling the Camino was 'religious', 'religious and other', or 'other'. In the case of 'religious' or 'religious and other' a compostela is available; in the case of 'other' there is a simpler certificate in Spanish."

So, if you think this walk is for you, my advice is to do lots of research and preparation first. As you walk along on your own pilgrimage, perhaps it is worth contemplating what you wish to do when moving forward with your life.

Bare This in Mind When Making that Life-Changing Decision

"At this time, it was just a dream. But the more we thought about it, the more the idea appealed to us. This was a big decision. Huge. Enormous. Many friends just thought we were completely mad to even consider it. Giving up your home and a way of life that is considered ordinary or normal is not a decision to be taken lightly. Most people aspire to realising their dreams – whatever they may be – when they retire. However, we have known and heard of many people who did not reach retirement age or were not in good enough health by that time to carry through their plans. We have always held a philosophy that we should live life to the full and make the most of whatever time we have. This is not morbid, but common sense and there are far too many people who wish they had the courage and bravery to realise their dream before it's too late." **ISN'T IT COLD IN WINTER? – BY KAREN WILES – AMAZON BOOKS**

Walk the walk…

Comments:

One thought on "The Camino de Santiago"

Frankie Moor

JUNE 10th 2018 AT 5:25 P.M.

One of my friends did the whole walk. As she did so she carried a list of people's names with her in her rucksack. People she wanted to carry on her journey. I was one of the names and yet we have only ever met through our Facebook contact (I am an advocate of social media; as long as it is used responsibly). She is a "lone" traveller in the world and her bravery is humbling. I will introduce you via fb. This trail would be incredible to do. As always… I feel inspired by you. Frankie xx

*

How to Find Freedom, Peace and Happiness

Blog Post JUNE 17th 2018

Bravery = Happiness

"We have no reason to mistrust our world, for it is not against us. Has it terrors, they are our terrors: has it abysses, those abysses belong to us; are dangers at hand, we must try to love them… How should we be able to forget those ancient myths about dragons that at the last moment turn into princesses; perhaps all the dragons of our lives are princesses who are only waiting to see us once beautiful and brave." **RAINER MARIA RILKE, LETTERS TO A YOUNG POET**

Happiness = Bravery

Why do I say this? Why do I believe this with all my heart; because this is how I completely turned things around for me.

I'm happy!!! Yes, I am finally happy and content, deep in my heart. I can actually say I have fallen back in love with myself again; something I thought would never happen. I have been able to achieve this through the recognition that I had stopped being myself; that I was pretending to be someone else and it was that which was making me unhappy.

I am aware from talking to other like-minded people that I am not alone in this; I think many of us are living a life of conformity, of doing what is expected from us by our peers, our employers and by society in general. My happiest years in the past were when I was living a crazy life in my youth. My hair was all the colours of the rainbow and my clothes were flamboyant and eccentric. I frequented clubs full of hippies and world music fans and I saw lots of live music. I was comfortable being 'me'.

But as I grew older, I started conforming to society and I cut my hair, shaved off my beard and started wearing conservative clothes. Over the years I had become lost in work and forgotten about who I really was.

It has only been since an enlightened moment in India that I was able to say to myself, "What happened to you? Where has the real you gone?"

"Doing what you like is freedom. Liking what you do is happiness." **Frank Tyger**

I realised that for the last few years I had been trying to be another person, listening to my mother and my colleagues who would say, "I prefer your hair short like that," or "your beard needs a trim," and I would think, oh yes, I will do that when I get home. I stopped going out because the places I was going to were simply not who I really was; I was bored with them.

Then one day I found myself in a hippie club in Goa and felt a wave of happiness; I was amongst my own and it felt right. I danced all night and I met some amazing people. For the first time in decades, I felt that warm glow of happiness and elation.

It felt so right but there was something very wrong. Everybody there, of every age and race, with their beaming faces and warm embraces, were dressed in flamboyant garb, beads and colourful clothes, their hair long and wild; they were being their true selves. And in the centre of it all was me, dressed like an American tourist, in chinos and a blue suit shirt and smart shoes: who the fuck was that??? Not me, what the hell had happened to me? What in god's name had I been thinking all those years?

I felt angry at myself. It was a true awakening!

"Dream as if you'll live forever, live as if you'll die today." **James Dean**

At 52 years old I decided from that day on I would go back to being the person I really was and I don't just mean looking how I wanted to look, but also to live the life I wanted to live; to grab that dream of living on a canal boat six months of the year and living in Goa for the rest of the year. To embrace the hippie I always was and stop being somebody else. I stupidly thought I was unhappy because I was overweight, old and unattractive, but it simply took my accepting who I really was to make me happy.

Now, I don't give a shit if I'm a bit fat or older because I am being real and true to myself and I feel great! But this transformation from a grey moth to bright butterfly can involve a lot of bravery.

So, if you have ever wished you could be the person you really want to be but don't because of work, or family or peer pressure; heed my words, this will only lead to unhappiness. If you secretly wish you could have a Mohican hairstyle with a stud in your nose but feel you can't because the world would call you weird; tell the world to go to hell and just do it. If you want to grow your hair and beard long and take off on a motorbike around the world; just do it. If you want to move to a hippie commune in a forest and live off the earth; just do it and stop conforming.

So, my answer to how to find Happiness, Peace and Freedom is to find the 'true you' and to be that person, not society's version of who you should be. Once you are being true to yourself and living the life you really want to live, happiness will follow.

LIFE IS FOR LIVING!!!

75 Thoughts on Happiness

1. "Dream as if you'll live forever, live as if you'll die today." James Dean
2. "Doing what you like is freedom. Liking what you do is happiness." Frank Tyger
3. "Be happy with what you have. Be excited about what you want." Alan Cohen
4. "Life is a journey, and if you fall in love with the journey, you will be in love forever." Peter Hagerty
5. "I've learned that people will forget what you said, people will forget what you did, but people will never forget how you made them feel." Maya Angelou
6. "Much of the stress that people feel doesn't come from having too much to do. It comes from not finishing what they've started." David Allen
7. "We forge the chains we wear in life." Charles Dickens
8. "If you look to others for fulfilment, you will never be fulfilled. If your happiness depends on money, you will never be happy with yourself. Be

content with what you have; rejoice in the way things are. When you realize there is nothing lacking, the world belongs to you." Lao Tzu

9. "Everything is a gift of the universe – even joy, anger, jealousy, frustration, or separateness. Everything is perfect either for our growth or our enjoyment." Ken Keyes Jr.
10. "There is no such thing as a problem without a gift for you in its hands. You seek problems because you need their gifts." Richard Bach
11. "If you want to be happy, set a goal that commands your thoughts, liberates your energy, and inspires your hopes." Andrew Carnegie
12. "Tension is who you think you should be; relaxation is who you are." Chinese Proverb
13. "For me it is sufficient to have a corner by my hearth, a book, and a friend, and a nap undisturbed by creditors or grief." Fernandez de Andrada
14. "You cannot judge what should bring others joy, and others cannot judge what should bring you joy." Alan Cohen
15. "The art of living lies less in eliminating our troubles than growing with them." Bernard M. Baruch
16. "Our capacity to draw happiness from aesthetic objects or material goods in fact seems critically dependent on our first satisfying a more important range of emotional or psychological needs, among them the need for understanding, for love, expression and respect." Alain De Botton
17. "If you start to think the problem is 'out there', stop yourself. That thought is the problem." Stephen Covey
18. "Happiness cannot be travelled to, owned, earned, worn or consumed. Happiness is the spiritual experience of living every minute with love, grace, and gratitude." Denis Waitley
19. "Happiness is not a station you arrive at, but a manner of traveling." Margaret Lee Runbeck
20. "Security is when everything is settled, when nothing can happen to you; security is the denial of life." Germaine Greer
21. "Focus on the journey, not the destination. Joy is found not in finishing an activity but in doing it." Greg Anderson

22. "Thousands of candles can be lit from a single candle, and the life of the candle will not be shortened. Happiness never decreases by being shared." Buddha
23. "The best remedy for those who are afraid, lonely or unhappy is to go outside, somewhere where they can be quiet, alone with the heavens, nature and God. As long as this exists, and it certainly always will, then there will be comfort for every sorrow, whatever the circumstances may be." Anne Frank
24. "In our lives, change is unavoidable, loss is unavoidable. In the adaptability and ease with which we experience change, lies our happiness and freedom." Buddha
25. "Live with intention. Walk to the edge. Listen hard. Practice wellness. Play with abandon. Laugh. Choose with no regret. Do what you love. Live as if this is all there is." Mary Anne Roadacher-Hershey
26. "You never regret being kind." Nicole Shepherd
27. "They who can give up essential liberty to obtain a little temporary safety, deserve neither liberty nor safety." Ben Franklin
28. "Forgiveness does not change the past, but it does enlarge the future." Paul Boese
29. "The secret of health for both mind and body is not to mourn for the past, worry about the future, or anticipate troubles, but to live in the present moment wisely and earnestly." Buddha
30. "True happiness is not attained through self-gratification, but through fidelity to a worthy purpose." Helen Keller
31. "Money is neither my god nor my devil. It is a form of energy that tends to make us more of who we already are, whether it's greedy or loving." Dan Millman
32. "The need for forgiveness is an illusion. There is nothing to forgive." Rachel England
33. "Blessed are those who can give without remembering and take without forgetting." Bernard Meltzer
34. "Reflect upon your present blessings, of which every man has many – not on your past misfortunes, of which all men have some." Charles Dickens
35. "Even a happy life cannot be without a measure of darkness, and the word happy would lose its meaning if it were not balanced by sadness.

It is far better to take things as they come along with patience and equanimity." Carl Jung

36. "He who lives in harmony with himself lives in harmony with the universe." Marcus Aurelius
37. "If you want others to be happy, practice compassion. If you want to be happy, practice compassion." Dalai Lama
38. "When one door of happiness closes, another opens, but often we look so long at the closed door that we do not see the one that has been opened for us." Helen Keller
39. "Happiness is not having what you want. It is appreciating what you have." Unknown
40. "True happiness… arises, in the first place, from the enjoyment of one's self." Joseph Addison
41. "Happiness is that state of consciousness which proceeds from the achievement of one's values." AynRand
42. "Most of us are just about as happy as we make up our minds to be." William Adams
43. "Success is getting what you want. Happiness is wanting what you get." Dale Carnegie
44. "We can have peace if we let go of wanting to change the past and wanting to control the future." Lester Levinson
45. "We make a living by what we get, we make a life by what we give." Winston Churchill
46. "Money doesn't bring happiness and creativity. Your creativity and happiness brings money." Sam Rosen
47. "Happiness is the experience of loving life. Being happy is being in love with that momentary experience. And love is looking at someone or even something and seeing the absolute best in him/her or it. Love is happiness with what you see. So love and happiness really are the same thing… just expressed differently." Robert McPhillips
48. "Everything that irritates us about others can lead us to an understanding of ourselves." Carl Jung
49. "God, grant me the serenity to accept the things I cannot change, the courage to change the things I can, and the wisdom to know the difference." Reinhold Niebuhr

50. "I am not bound to win, I am bound to be true. I am not bound to succeed, but I am bound to live up to the light I have." Abraham Lincoln
51. "Gratitude unlocks the fullness of life. It turns what we have into enough, and more. It turns denial into acceptance, chaos to order, confusion to clarity. It can turn a meal into a feast, a house into a home, a stranger into a friend. Gratitude makes sense of our past, brings peace for today, and creates a vision for tomorrow." Melody Beattie
52. "There is no stress in the world, only people thinking stressful thoughts and then acting on them." Wayne Dyer
53. "We all get report cards in many different ways, but the real excitement of what you're doing is in the doing of it. It's not what you're gonna get in the end – it's not the final curtain – it's really in the doing it, and loving what you're doing." Ralph Lauren
54. "In the midst of movement and chaos, keep stillness inside of you." Deepak Chopra
55. "Success at the highest level comes down to one question: Can you decide that your happiness can come from someone else's success?" Bill Walton If you can, you take the most important step towards becoming a great leader.
56. "There is only one thing more painful than learning from experience and that is not learning from experience." Archibald McLeish
57. "Once you do something you love, you never have to work again." Willie Hill
58. "Anything in life that we don't accept will simply make trouble for us until we make peace with it." Shakti Gawain
59. "The right way is not always the popular and easy way. Standing for right when it is unpopular is a true test of moral character." Margaret Chase Smith
60. "Persons of high self-esteem are not driven to make themselves superior to others; they do not seek to prove their value by measuring themselves against a comparative standard. Their joy is being who they are, not in being better than someone else." Nathaniel Branden
61. "Anxiety is the dizziness of freedom." Soren Kierkegaard
62. "Do what you have always done and you'll get what you have always got." Sue Knight

63. "The happiness of life is made up of the little charities of a kiss or smile, a kind look, a heartfelt compliment." Samuel Taylor Coleridge
64. "We avoid the things that we're afraid of because we think there will be dire consequences if we confront them. But the truly dire consequences in our lives come from avoiding things that we need to learn about or discover." Shakti Gawain
65. "Think of what you have rather than of what you lack. Of the things you have, select the best and then reflect how eagerly you would have sought them if you did not have them." Marcus Aurelius
66. "Happiness is where we find it, but very rarely where we seek it." Petit Senn
67. "To be content means that you realize you contain what you seek." Alan Cohen
68. "The mind is its own place, and in itself can make a heaven of hell, a hell of heaven." John Milton
69. "In our daily lives, we must see that it is not happiness that makes us grateful, but the gratefulness that makes us happy." Albert Clarke
70. "Look at everything as though you were seeing it either for the first or last time. Then your time on earth will be filled with glory." Betty Smith
71. "You are responsible for your life. You can't keep blaming somebody else for your dysfunction. Life is really about moving on." Oprah Winfrey
72. "Expecting life to treat you well because you are a good person is like expecting an angry bull not to charge because you are a vegetarian." Shari R. Barr
73. "View your life from your funeral, looking back at your life experiences, what have you accomplished? What would you have wanted to accomplish but didn't? What were the happy moments? What were the sad? What would you do again, and what you wouldn't?" Victor Frankl
74. "Far better is it to dare mighty things, to win glorious triumphs – even though checked by failure – than to rank with those poor spirits who neither enjoy much nor suffer much, because they live in a grey twilight that knows not victory nor defeat." Theodore Roosevelt
75. "Boredom is the feeling that everything is a waste of time… serenity, that nothing is." Thomas Szasz

The Significance of Happiness in Hinduism

Source: www.hinduwebsite.com

By **Jayaram V**

"Existence; for truly on obtaining the delight of existence one becomes blissful (Taittiriya Upanishad, 2.7.1.).

Peace arises from cultivating friendship with those who are happy, compassion towards those who are in distress, joy towards those who are virtuous, and sameness towards those who are not virtuous (Yogasutras, 1.33).

According to Hinduism, happiness in human life arises mainly from one's own actions, past life karma, actions of gods and others, and the grace of God."

In Hindu scriptures we find references to mainly three types of happiness as stated below.

1. Physical **(bhautika)** happiness, or **sukham,** which arises from comforts of life, sensual enjoyment, and bodily pleasures.
2. Mental **(manasika)** happiness, or **anandam**, which arises from sense of **fulfillment** and freedom from worries, afflictions, and anxieties.
3. Spiritual **(adhyatmika)** happiness, or **atmanandam**, which arises from freedom from the cycle of births and deaths, and union with Self.

"According to Hinduism, an embodied being's ultimate purpose is **enjoyment** of supreme bliss as a free soul **(mukta)** in the highest heaven. Enjoyment is also the basis of happiness upon earth. However, in mortal life happiness should not be pursued for happiness' sake alone, because **mere** pursuit of happiness in a bound state **(baddha)** leads to attachment (Yogasutras 2.7), and bondage. It should be pursued as part of a way of life in which liberation or union with the Self should be the highest goal."

Comments:

One thought on "How to find Freedom Peace and Happiness"

David

JUNE 18th 2018 AT 1:27 P.M.

The comments are so true – it's starting the journey and being mindful of who you are and keeping hold of it that I find the hardest, but it will happen and maybe I will find my inner hippy too!

*

I hope you have enjoyed these excerpts from my blog and I invite you to take a look if you are looking for ways of moving on from a full stop life and finding hippie happiness: **hippiekushiwakinguptolife.com**

*

Conclusion

I am sitting here at my computer typing out this last chapter. It's late October 2019 and outside its dark, even though its 9:50 a.m. in the morning – the sky is grey and it's raining and cold, but I'm warm inside. Last weekend was Whirl-y-Gig and my whole crew was out having a fantastic time. I've managed to break my foot in a silly accident which involved a cup of tea and a sofa (don't ask) but it didn't stop me from going to Whirly. It was a great night, with loads of bongo drummers, lots of hippies dancing around like crazed aliens and there was even someone dressed in a massive dinosaur costume. I flirted with a handsome young man and talked him into taking his top off (cheap thrills, naughty boy). At the end of the night Louise reminded me she loved me and how happy she was we are friends.

Yesterday she invited me to the Blue Orchid bar in Surbiton Surrey. We did shots and later went back to hers for some wine and a smoke, it was lovely. I managed to convince her to save up and come to Goa with me in February. Las is hopefully coming too and Tracy; it's going to be spectacular!

It seems apt then that we end this first book the way we began it, in Goa. I have a big, five-week trip planned and it is going to be special; so who cares if it's cold and grey outside, I am warm and positively glowing.

*

Prologue
Goa; a Pilgrimage of Meditation and Rebuilding

"The sun was slowly rising behind the palm trees, their black silhouettes against the orange sunrise. We walked back along the beach. The ocean was calm that day and the jungle of Goa was slowly waking up, with bird calls breaking up the silence, and with the leopard nowhere in sight. It was a low tide, ocean floor exposed, and the hard sand easy to walk on, with thousands of tiny little creeks forming on the beach as if the jungle floor was draining into the ocean. On the way back, we had to cross a river, rivulet actually, just a foot or two deep, a stream that cut our path along the beach." On the Road Again – Dragan Ralulovich

Goa is my happy place – when I'm there I feel elated and alive, ready for anything and I dream about the future and its possibilities.

When I'm at home in the UK and it's raining or I'm feeling down, I think about dancing on Arambol beach with the hippies; and I smile inside, knowing it won't be long.

> "I used to hate it when people used to ask me:
> **What are you running from?**
> I used to protest that I was running to things – mountains, parties, deserts, islands, adventures – things most people dreamed of.
> I wanted to live in the dream."
> **Tales of a Road Junky – Tom Thumb**

Goa changed my life – it made me the hippie Kushi person I am today; it woke me up and made me happy again.

I love the markets and the crazy bars, I love the trance parties but most of all I love the people, the locals but also the people I meet from all over the world; it's wonderful.

"I don't know if we ever really find ourselves. Each time we think we have it all worked out it seems to slip through our fingers. But I do know that meeting ourselves is a journey we make every day – but then it's no longer about running away, it's coming back home." Tales of a Road Junky – Tom Thumb

On January 20th 2020 (seems the number 20 is significant on this trip) I am travelling to Goa on a five-week trip that will be something a little different from my previous visits to India.

Normally for me, it would be all about party, party, party, with a few touristy things thrown in but on this trip, I am spending the first week in the South with my good friend Geoff in an area called Benaulim. This is quite a quiet laid-back area and I intend to fill this time with rest, meditation, yoga and swimming. I really need that mind cleaning time after a difficult year.

I have been coping with a cough and chest infection that has been reoccurring several times over the year. It turns out I have had a reflux issue which has finally been diagnosed and I now take pills for it and it has now completely cleared up. But this has been tiring and depressing and has messed up my plans this year a lot.

As soon as this health problem was resolved I have managed to break my foot. So, you can see I really need some time out.

A Beach in Benaulim

After Benaulim, I am moving on to Palolem also in the South of Goa. Palolem is famous for its beautiful beaches and beach huts on stilts. It's a bit busier than Benaulim but still fairly quiet and peaceful. This is said to be a good spot to go out and see dolphins and other wildlife.

There are lots of retreats there and places to do yoga, have a massage and to meditate. This will be the second part of my meditation rest and recuperation before the madness of the North of the state.

Palolem

"The resident characters that really made the ambience in Goa were the animals. There were vagabond cows who ate the flowers off roadside shrines and who chased you for your bananas on the beach. Sometimes the beach dogs would hassle them and they'd break into a run, sending people diving out of the way."
Tales of a Road Junky – Tom Thumb

"The beach dogs themselves were a motley crew of canines in varying degrees of health. Some of them were mangy beyond hope and they gave birth to pitiful batches of puppies that would never survive the rainy season. One night I was tripping with a friend on the beach, staring at images of Shiva dancing in the moonlight on the waves. We slowly became aware of a paw that had landed on each of our shoulders as one of the mongrels had come to pay homage, too." Tales of a Road Junky – Tom Thumb

After this replenishing time in the South, I will take the train up North to Anjuna. I love this area with its wonderful Wednesday market, its trance parties and ocean-side bars; it is full of life and vibrancy.

I intend to find accommodation once I get there and probably go on a few tours out of the beach resorts. The temple tour and spice farm is always a good day out.

I find the food at the beach shacks in Anjuna is pretty good and the bars are a great place to meet new people. Then it's a case of keeping your ears open for the next party; and party I will.

"The snakes were an abstract concept until you actually saw one. After that you didn't walk barefoot at night any more. A snake bite could cripple you for life or even kill and so it was a good plan to stamp your feet as you walked and use a torch to see the small ones that were too slow to get out of the way." Tales of a Road Junky – Tom Thumb

"In India you ended up believing everything!"
Tales of a Road Junky – Tom Thumb

The exciting thing about this part of the journey is many of you crazy people are coming over to Goa and out to Anjuna at this time because of Hilltop festival. I am so looking forward to hooking up with people like my good friends Louise, Las and Mellissa.

Hilltop is the big event of this period – it's a trance party and it's going to be wild. Who wouldn't want to be dancing amongst the palm trees under a tropical moon?

After the craziness of Anjuna, my final week will be in my happy place: Arambol.

Home of the hippies, the drum circles, yoga and Tai Chi, meditation and all-night hippie parties, I love it. These feel like my people and it is here my Hippie Kushi journey began; oh, and there's some really good restaurants and a great market there too.

I need this little pilgrimage of meditation and rebuilding:

Goa Is Coming and I Can't Wait!

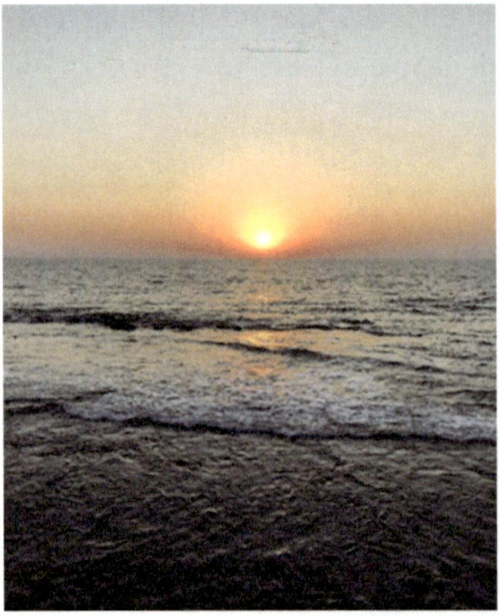

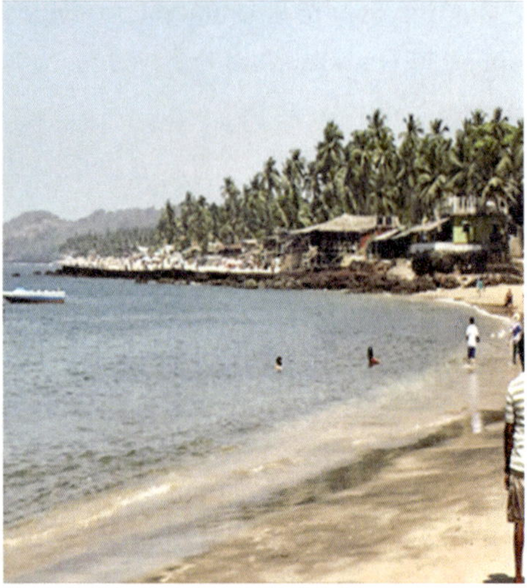

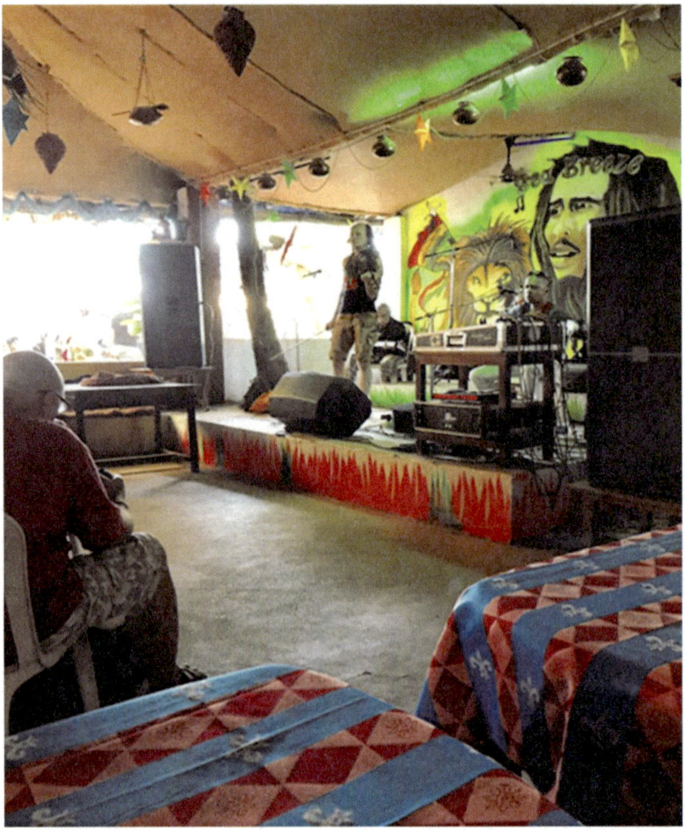
Breeze

I hope you have taken something from our first adventure into hippie happiness. Everyone has the potential to change their life, surroundings, and happiness! In book two I will be exploring the environment and how we live our lives as well as what we eat and how it affects the planet. I also want to look at long term vagabonding travel and the global nomad lifestyle and how that can alter our mind-set forever. Finally, I would like to explore spirituality and meditation in more detail as well as self-confidence and being brave in order to be who we really are.

I have covered many elements in this first book: most importantly how to take control of our own lives, being who we should be in the form of our 'true-selves' and bringing out our wonderful creative side.

We have explored how looking at the best parts of our lives and rekindling them is not about living in the past but simply remembering what used to make us happy before we got stuck in a full stop existence and seeing if it is possible to rekindle a part of that today; like I did with Whirl-y-Gig and travel.

We looked at how travelling the world, visiting places like India, especially Goa and beautiful countries like Thailand and Vietnam, broadens our horizons, moving us away from that package holiday mentality, towards a more life-affirming, adventure-filled, life-changing experience.

I spoke with joy about how dancing to wonderful music with other like-minded people can uplift us, bond us with others and fill us with elation; you will never feel old again. By getting out there you will find new exciting friends and that will lead to new and exciting places and experiences.

I hope you can find a way, regardless of which country you live in, to regularly attend Whirl-y-Gig and Whirl-y-Fayre (even if it's only once a year) it will change your life. You will feel part of a loving, joyful family.

Wherever you are, it is so important to regularly attend festivals – they are full of love, wonderful music, camaraderie and togetherness. That feeling will make you want to embrace your Hippie Kushi side.

You will start to feel happier and more connected to your new hippie self if you think about changing your mind-set and the way you look at the world and the way you live your life. Embrace life and expand your hippie consciousness.

Love your fellow man (and woman) and your planet.

You should think seriously about adopting an alternative lifestyle – consider moving onto a canal boat or into a community coop, travelling Europe in your full-time campervan home or joining a hippie community.

Live a life full of Hippie Kushi, doing what you want to do!!!

I hope all of this information has helped wake you up and I hope my own personal story and insight has helped you to start contemplating a new you; a Hippie Kushi you. Your life can be full of hippie happiness; you just need to wake up to life!

Hippie Kushi Wake Up to Life...

Letter from a Reader:

Hi, Hippie Kushi! I just came across your blog and really liked your ideas and was impressed by the changes you are making in your life! I'm 19 and I have always viewed life from a philosophical perspective. At times this was very hard because I saw life through an existential lens, different from the way you see it I think, in which life and the universe existed separately from myself. I felt lost, alone, and struggled with the meaning of my life. This year I started practising sgi Buddhism and it changed my life! I truly had a human revolution! I stepped out of my comfort zone, talked to more people, and made many friends! It changed my life! I completely agree with your statement that everyone has the potential to change their life, surroundings, and happiness! Thank you for sharing this wisdom on your blog!

BOOK TWO OUT SOON (once I've written it)

*

Quotes

- The Fairy Gathering – Poem by Blushfulmoon: https://allpoetry.com/Blushfulmoon
- Bedroll, Bushes and Beeches – The Hippie Years – Ron White – Published January 7th 2019 by Flower Power Press
- The Owl and the Pussycat – Edward Lear – 1812–1888
- In Search of the Lost Chord 1967 and the idea – Danny Goldberg – ICON books ltd 2017
- The Hippies a 1960S History – John Anthony Morella-Publisher McFarland & Co Inc. Publication date 28 Feb 2017
- Hinduism for Beginners – Shalu Sharma – Abebooks – 2016
- http://www.religionfacts.com/vishnu
- Planet Backpacker-Robert Downes – Wandering Press 2008
- From Heartbreak to the Hippie Trail – Kenneth Liss – July 27th 2018 – KIM Publishing
- Source: www.vice.com
- Source: www.discogs.com
- How to Live in a Van and Travel – Mike Hudson – 2017 – Bluedog Books
- Adam Bloodworth of the METRO newspaper wrote this article for Metro news- https://metro.co.uk/2017/08/04/wilderness-festival-our-pick-of-what-not-to-miss-at-oxfordshires-luxurious-summer-festival-6830350/ – Friday 4 Aug 2017 11:52 p.m.
- Star Trek's 50-year mission: to shine a light on the best of humankind By Dave Schilling: The Observer- https://www.theguardian.com/culture/2016/sep/04/star-trek--50-year-mission-best-of-humankind – Sun 4 Sep 2016 07.00 BST Last modified on Thu 22 Feb 2018 20.40 GMT

- Quotes courtesy of www.abhota.info
- Journeys in the Kali Yuga: A Pilgrimage from Esoteric India to Pagan Europe
- Aki Cederberg – Publisher: Destiny Books; 1 edition (12 Dec. 2017)
- Kaleidoscope City – Piers Moore Ede – Bloomsbury Publishing; 1 edition (26 Feb. 2015)
- Page 50: Hinduism for idiots – Linda Johnsen – Publisher: Alpha; 2nd ed. edition (May 5th 2009)
- Karma Article source: berkleycenter.georgetown.edu
- Global Nomads, Techno and New Age as Transnational Countercultures in Ibiza and Goa: Routledge; 1st edition (April 6th 2007) Anthony D'Andrea
- Hippie is a state of mind – Source: Living at latitude 38 and 61- https://livingatlatitude38and61.wordpress.com/2012/10/18/hippie-is-a-state-of-mind/
- 8 Ways to Ignite Your Inner Happiness-Claire Charters – Source: www.mindbodygreen.com
- Global Nomads, Techno and New Age as Transnational Countercultures in Ibiza and Goa: Routledge; 1st edition (April 6th 2007) Anthony D'Andrea
- Source: www.theschooloflife.com- https://www.theschooloflife.com/thebookoflife/the-true-and-the-false-self/
- Source: theconversation.com-http://theconversation.com/five-reasons-why-being-kind-makes-you-feel-good-according-to-science-92459
- Source: medium.com
- Source: nationalcooperativelawcenter.com- http://nationalcooperativelawcenter.com/national-cooperative-law-center/the-history-of-housing-cooperatives/
- Source: www.thegoodtrade.com- https://www.thegoodtrade.com/features/5-reasons-to-consider-joining-a-cohousing-community
- Source: www.independent.co.uk- https://www.independent.co.uk/property/house-and-home/come-together-could-communal-living-be-the-solution-to-our-housing-crisis-6260020.html

- Lee Carroll quoted in the book – The Gaia Effect – Kryon Monika Muranyi – Publisher: Ariane Editions (4 Aug. 2014)
- The Pros and Cons of Living Afloat – www.waterways.org.uk – Created on 14/10/2014 – https://www.waterways.org.uk/blog/pros_cons_living_afloat
- Hero for High Times by Ian Marchant – Vintage books – Jonathan Cape London – January 15th 2018
- Exert taken from The News Minute – Friday, September 2nd 2016
- Source: hippie-inheels.com
- Source: theplaidzebra.com
- Source: www.goavilla.co.uk/goa
- George Santayana – 'The Philosophy of Travel'- Taken from The Birth of Reason and Other Essays
- Camino Adventures-www.caminoadventures.com/reasons-walk-camino-de-santiago
- Rainer Maria Rilke, Letters to a Young Poet- Publisher: W. W. Norton & Company; Revised edition (17 Sept. 1993)
- Isn't it Cold in Winter? – by Karen Wiles – Amazon Books
- The significance of Happiness in Hinduism Source: www.hinduwebsite.com By Jayaram V
- On the Road Again – Dragan Ralulovich – Publisher: CreateSpace Independent Publishing Platform (January 23rd 2018)
- Tales of a Road Junky – Tom Thumb – Amazon Books – Published (first published February 9th 2011)
- Blog: Hippiekushiwakinguptolife.com
- Facebook: Hippie Kushi Waking Up to Life